# Divine Epicure's

## Recipe Book and Nutritional Guide

# Divine Epicure's

## Recipe Book and Nutritional Guide

*Healthy and Tasty Recipes for Vegetarians and Non-Vegetarians*

Greta Andrews

AuthorHouse™
1663 Liberty Drive
Bloomington, IN 47403
www.authorhouse.com
Phone: 1-800-839-8640

First published by AuthorHouse    05/10/2011

ISBN: 9781463400521 (sc)
ISBN: 9781463400545 (dj)
ISBN: 9781463400538 (ebk)

Library of Congress Control Number: 2011907970

Printed in the United States of America

Any people depicted in stock imagery provided by Thinkstock are models, and such images are being used for illustrative purposes only.
All photography by: SirHarold Vives Mojica.

This book is printed on acid-free paper.

# Special Thanks and Acknowledgements

## Honor

This book is in honor of our Creator, who created everything through Jesus Christ. He created us all fearfully and wonderfully. He has given us wonderful food and all of His creation to enjoy. God, our Creator, is the Divine Epicure. I am just His instrument to give this to you. I pray that everything that He has given me to give you in this book will be a blessing to you and your family.

## Dedication

I dedicate this book to my son, Chris, to my daughter-in-law, Tammy, to my granddaughter, TiAna, to my grandson, Davian and to my grandson, Bryson, who is in heaven. My desire is that all that I have is imparted to you to enjoy the abundant life that has been provided for you.

## Thanks

I want to thank everyone who has been supportive of me with this project. Especially the one who has been there every step of the way. And to everyone who has assisted, prayed and encouraged me, I love you and thank you with all my heart.

# Contents

# Preface

This book contains a variety of recipes that I have created. It also contains a wealth of nutritional information on many fruits, vegetables, herbs, nuts, seeds and other foods. This information has been gathered from different books and resources listed in the back of this book. The information from the references used is primarily based on research.

It states in the Holy Bible, Genesis 1: 29 *"And God said, 'See, I have given you every herb that yields seed which is on the face of the earth, and every tree whose fruit yields seed; to you it shall be for food.'"* As research is being done on plant food, the researchers are finding that the health and healing attributes of these foods are endless. One awesome discovery after another is being revealed about what our Creator provided for us to live healthy and wholesome lives. We need to take advantage of what He has given us to live healthier lives. I hope that what I am sharing with you in this book will help you to do this.

I encourage you to check out the resources that I have listed in the back of this book and acquire even more knowledge than what I have provided to you. We can help our physicians out by making sure that we are maintaining a healthy diet, taking vitamin supplements and exercising on a regular basis. We should all be knowledgeable about our bodies and what we need to keep ourselves healthy. I have made that a mission of my own for the past thirty years with a desire to keep my health and wellness in my own hands. In the course of life, I have encountered a health issue due to the affects of getting older. Knowing what I know is what has kept and is keeping me alive. I hope that you will benefit from this information in the same way.

# Introduction

I love to cook! I love to put good tasty foods together. I also have a passion about the great nutritional benefits that we have in many fruits, vegetables, nuts, herbs and seeds. After reading about all of the amazing nutritional and healing foods that are available to us from our Creator, I have become dedicated to coming up with new and exciting ways to prepare foods that are high in nutritional value and make them taste great. As I began to do this for myself, I started sharing my creations with friends. That grew into me sharing them with many different people and sharing the nutritional information with them also. That is the reason that I am writing this book today. The sharing is just continuing on with you. I hope that this book will help you to create more healthy foods that you will enjoy and that will help you and your family to maintain good health as our Creator intended.

We have so many wonderful fruits, vegetables, nuts, seeds and herbs available to us that are full of great vitamins and minerals that are so delicious and beautiful! I have so much fun coming up with new ways to mix these together. After each recipe I have shared just a little nugget of health information about one or two ingredients. More information is provided in the Nutritional Guide section of this book. It is my desire that we all become more practical about preparing our food in a more healthy way that is better for us on a daily basis.

We have many health experts telling us that we should eat more carrots, kale, beets, etc. While we do become fascinated with the awesome information about the outstanding health and healing qualities of foods like these, we usually quickly go back to the old unhealthy ways of eating. We are spoiled as a society to enjoying more palatable foods that are not always good for us. I hope that this book will help you to do what the doctor has order. Who said healthy has to be tasteless and boring? Because I love to prepare and enjoy spicy and scrumptious dishes, I have come up with different ways that I can enjoy these healthy foods that the doctor has ordered in a way that I am accustomed. The techniques are also practical so that they can become a way of life and not just a quick healthy phase.

Every fruit, vegetable, nut, seed and herb has unique nutritional and healing qualities in them. Research has been done that we all rely on to tell us what they have been created do. I have taken to heart the information that I have read and heard from selected and reliable resources. I have found this information to be most helpful in preventing disease and aiding in any medical care when I do have an illness. In this book I will share some of that information and my resources for that information.

This book will give you a variety of ways to prepare different foods. The different salads, salsas, juices, smoothies and sandwiches will give you the opportunity to consume your fruits, vegetables, nuts and seeds in a raw state. This is usually the best way to eat them. When they are live, the life giving qualities in them are alive and enhancing your life with those qualities. While these recipes are unique, they are still practical enough for you to just buy the ingredients from your local grocer. There are certain ingredients that are used repeatedly so that you don't have to spend a lot of money and you can easily make this way of cooking a lifestyle for you. I encourage you to take these ideas and create your own recipes that are more healthy yet enjoyable in taste.

I will get you started with some helpful hints. We will then get into the recipes. The second half of this book will give you some nutritional information, then eating plans and wrapping it up with an Eating Plan Worksheet. I hope that you will find this book to be helpful, life changing and inspiring. This is not a recipe book to look pretty on display in your kitchen. This is to be a tool for you to improve your health and quality of life on a daily basis.

Now let's get started!

# Let's Get Started!

I want to share some of my cooking techniques and cooking tools that I use to cook and prepare food. You may already use these same techniques or tools. If so, that is great! If not, I hope that this information will be helpful to you.

**What You Need To Get Started**

**Blender**—The blender will puree and liquefy foods. It will also be used to make your delicious smoothies.

**Brush**—You need a good brush to thoroughly wash your fruits and vegetables. It will help to remove dirt, pesticides and wax.

**Citrus juicer**—This juicer is best for lemon, orange and grapefruit juicing.

**Colander**—The colander is very helpful when washing vegetables, fruits and any food in the sink. It keeps the food from touching the sink which can be unsanitary. It also keeps them from falling down the drain.

**Cutting Board**—Cutting boards come in plastic and wood. I use both. But you have to be careful with the cutting on boards made out of wood. As you continue to use them, splinters will develop and can get mixed up in your food.

**Graduated measuring cups (½ cup, ¼ cup, etc.)**—Even though your 1 cup measuring cup will have these measured out, it is still good to have separate little cups for each amount.

**Grater**—In addition to grating cheese, this will be used to create lemon and orange zests.

**Juicer**—I recommend investing into a good juicer for your vegetables and fruits.

**Knives**—You really need a good set of knives with a good sharpener. This would be a wise investment to be able to prepare your salads, salsas and meats without frustration.

**Measuring cup**—It is good to have different sizes from 1 cup up to 4 cups.

**Measuring spoons**—These usually come in a set of a few nested spoons and can start as low as 1/8 teaspoon (t) and incrementally increase to 1 tablespoon (T).

**Mixer**—This appliance will be beneficial for mixing and whipping foods.

**Mixing bowls**—I recommend having at least a couple of large bowls and a set of graduated sizes.

**Spoons**—You will need a least a couple of very sturdy and large spoons with long handles for stir and mixing thoroughly.

**Vegetable wash**—I recommend keeping a good vegetable wash on hand to remove germs, pesticides and waxes from your fruits and vegetables.

**Whisk**—This instrument will be used to mix liquid and dry ingredients that don't need a mixer.

## *A New Practical Way of Cutting*

Most of the time when we eat a salad, we have to use a knife to cut the vegetables and fruit into smaller pieces in order to eat them properly and more conveniently. When I prepare salads, I prefer to cut them in a way that no more cutting is necessary while I am eating them. I have a particular way that I chop each ingredient. Most of them are listed below:

All leafy green vegetables, lettuce and cabbage—chop into ½ to 1 inch squares

Fruit—chop into ¼ inch squares or smaller, depending on the type of fruit

Carrots and beets—chop very fine

Cucumbers—dice into ¼ inch cubed squares

Cilantro and parsley—mince very finely

Nuts—chop into irregular pieces, if needed

Onions—mince

Bell peppers—mince

Tomatoes—dice into ¼—½ inch square

## *Helpful Chart*

| Action | Description | Foods |
|---|---|---|
| Caramelize | Cook until firm texture is converted to soft texture and slightly brown | Onions |
| Chop | Cut into moderate sized pieces, usually ½ inch or smaller squares | Leafy green vegetables, cabbage, lettuce |
| Finely Chop | Chop into fine pieces | Beets, carrots |
| Dice | Chop into small ¼ inch cubes | Cucumbers, tomatoes |
| Mince | Chop into fine irregular pieces | Onion, parsley, cilantro, dill |
| Sautee | Cook in small amount of oil or liquid until limp | Onion, green bell pepper, red bell, mushrooms, all vegetables and meats |

# Salsas

For many of my salads, I prepare different salsas that are blended into the salads or they can be used as a topping on the salad. All of these salsas can be eaten individually as a snack, with a salad or as a side dish with any meat or entree. The salsas are also great with chips. We will start with the Cucumber Salsa, since it is the first one that I created.

## Cucumber Salsa

3 cups cucumber, diced
½ cup red onion, finely chopped
½ cup cilantro, minced
4 oz. lemon juice
2 oz. olive oil
½ t sea salt

Thoroughly stir together all ingredients. For variety, you may add chopped avocado and tomatoes. This salsa can be the base ingredient of a variety of salsas. It is very refreshing. Be sure to adjust the recipe as desired to suit your taste to make it work for you. If the lemons are too tart, just add a little honey to balance it out.

*Nutritional note: Cucumbers are good for high and low blood pressures. They promote good health for your hair and nails. Onions are high in potassium. They are also good for your hair and nails. Lemon juice has so many nutritional benefits including fighting obesity, arthritis and liver ailments. Olive oil aids in releasing the phytochemicals and nutritional components from fruits and vegetables into our bodies.*

## *Corn Salsa*

6 cups raw corn, whole kernels
½ cup red pepper, diced
1 T jalapeno peppers, finely minced
½ cup red onion, minced
½ cup cilantro, minced
2 T olive oil
1 T lemon juice
½ t sea salt
½ t cayenne pepper
1 t garlic powder

Shave the corn kernels off each cob. Be careful not to shave too close to the cob, yet close enough to cut off the complete kernels. If the kernels have the dry white tips on the end, you have cut in too far. Mix kernels, red pepper, jalapeno peppers, onion and cilantro. Stir well. Pour in olive oil and lemon juice. Add sea salt, cayenne pepper and garlic powder. Adjust spice ingredients to taste.

Raw corn is so delicious and nutritious! This salsa is versatile and can be served in so many different ways, as a salsa, side dish, mixed with any of the salads or mixed with other vegetables to make a soup. It is also wonderful with the tortilla chips with a hint of jalapeno!

*Nutritional note: Corn promotes pancreatic health and aids in fighting anemia. Garlic fights high blood pressure and is a blood cleanser.*

## *Kale and Tomato Salsa*

2 cups kale, chopped very fine
1 cup tomatoes, diced
1 cup avocado, diced
1 cup carrots, finely chopped
1 cup pecans, chopped
2 T red onion, minced
2 T red bell pepper, minced

1 cup pomegranate seeds
½ cup cilantro, minced
2 T lemon juice
2 T olive oil
2 T garlic powder
½ t jalapeno pepper, minced
¼ t sea salt

Chop kale into ¼ inch or less squares. Mix kale, tomatoes, avocado, carrots, pecans, pomegranate seeds, onion, red bell pepper and cilantro together thoroughly. Add olive oil, jalapeno and seasonings.

**Nutritional note:** *Kale is very high in Vitamin A, Vitamin C and calcium. It fights obesity, arthritis, bladder ailment and diseases in the body. Tomatoes fight high blood pressure and infections. They improve skin and purify the blood. The nutritional benefits of carrots are endless, including being very high in Vitamin A, fighting obesity, toxemia, asthma, poor complexion, bladder problems and high blood pressure to name a few.*

## Kale and Olive Salsa

2 cups kale, chopped very fine
1 cup sun-dried tomatoes, chopped
1 cup kalamata olives, chopped
2 T parsley, minced
2 T red bell pepper, minced
2 T red onion, minced
1 T olive oil
1 T garlic powder
¼ t cayenne pepper
¼ t sea salt

Chop kale in ¼ inch or less squares. Mix kale, sun dried tomatoes, kalamata olives, parsley, red bell pepper and red onion together thoroughly. Add olive oil, garlic powder, cayenne pepper and sea salt. Mix thoroughly.

*Nutritional note:* *Parsley is very high in Vitamin A and calcium. It is valuable in cases of anemia, high blood pressure and arthritis. It fights diseases of the urinary tract. Cayenne pepper is good for digestion and high blood pressure.*

## Black Bean Salsa

1 can of black beans
1 medium jar chunky tomato salsa
2 cups of corn salsa (refer to Corn Salsa Recipe)

Open can of bean and drain off excess liquid. Add corn salsa and stir thoroughly. Add tomato salsa and stir thoroughly.

You may heat this salsa up and eat it as a soup. You may add whatever meat you would like or whatever other vegetable of your preference. This is so delicious and healthy!

*Nutritional note:* *Black beans are an excellent source iron, protein and fiber.*

## Artichoke and Spinach Salsa

2 cups artichoke hearts, chopped
2 cups spinach, raw and chopped
1 cup tomatoes, diced
1 cup avocado, diced
1 cup walnuts, chopped
½ cup red bell pepper, diced
2 T cilantro, minced
½ cup red onion, minced
2 T olive oil
2 T garlic powder
½ t sea salt
¼ t cayenne pepper

Chop artichoke hearts and spinach into ½ inch squares. Mix artichoke hearts, spinach, tomatoes, avocados, walnuts, red bell pepper, cilantro and red onion thoroughly. Add olive oil and seasonings. Mix thoroughly and enjoy with your favorite chips!

*Nutritional note: Artichokes are high in potassium. They aid in fighting anemia, rheumatism and granular disorders. Spinach is high in Vitamin A, Vitamin C and potassium. Spinach is another vegetable that has endless benefits such as fighting anemia, high blood pressure and bronchitis. And it aids in fighting kidney, bladder and liver ailments.*

## Artichoke and Tomato Salsa

2 cups artichoke hearts, chopped
1 cup tomatoes, chopped
1 cup red bell pepper, minced
1 cup parsley, minced
½ cup scallions, minced
2 T olive oil
2 T garlic powder
1 T basil flakes
1 t kelp
1 T lemon juice
½ t cayenne pepper
Pinch of sea salt

Mix artichoke hearts, tomatoes, bell pepper, parsley and scallions together. Stir thoroughly. Add oil, lemon juice and seasonings. Adjust seasonings to taste.

*Nutritional note: Kelp is a great salt substitute. It aids in digestion. It is also helpful in preventing and overcoming goiters. It fights anemia, impotency and helps to offset an inferior diet.*

## Artichoke and Olive Salsa

2 cups artichoke hearts, chopped
1 cup sun-dried tomatoes, chopped
½ cup kalamata olives, chopped
½ cup green olives, chopped
½ cup black olives, chopped
½ cup red bell pepper, minced
2 T cup red onion, thinly sliced and chopped
2 T olive oil
2 T garlic powder
½ t cayenne pepper
¼ t sea salt

Mix artichoke hearts, tomatoes, olives, bell pepper and onion. Stir thoroughly. Add olive oil and seasonings. Adjust seasonings to taste.

*Nutritional note: Olive oil stimulates contractions of the gall bladder. It is valuable for gall bladder health, helping to rid it of gall stones. Olives help to fight liver disorders, diabetes and indigestion problems.*

## Black Bean Artichoke Salsa

1 cup artichoke hearts, chopped
1 cup black beans, cooked and drained
1 cup raw tomatoes, diced
½ cup cilantro, minced
½ cup red bell pepper, minced
½ cup red onion, minced
1 T raw jalapeno, minced (optional)
2 T olive oil
2 T garlic powder
½ t sea salt

Mix artichoke hearts, black beans and tomatoes. Stir thoroughly. Add cilantro, bell pepper, onion. To ensure that the onion does not overpower the taste, add the onion a little at a time. If you don't use all of it, that is fine. Just save it for another dish. Add olive oil, garlic powder and sea salt.

*Nutritional note:* Cilantro helps to reduce the bad cholesterol and helps to increase the good cholesterol. It is high in anti-oxidants and aids in weight loss. Jalapenos contain a significant amount of Vitamin A.

## Cucumber and Celery Salsa

2 cups cucumbers, diced
1 cup tomatoes, diced
1 cup celery, diced
1 cup scallions, diced
1 cup red bell pepper, diced
½ cup cilantro, minced
2 T dill, minced
1 T no salt seasoning
1 T seaweed seasoning
2 T garlic powder
½ t paprika
¼ t sea salt
2 T lemon juice
2 T flaxseed oil

Mix cucumbers, tomatoes and celery. Stir thoroughly. Add scallions, red bell pepper and cilantro and dill. Stir thoroughly. Add seasonings. Stir thoroughly. Stir in lemon juice and flaxseed oil.

*Nutritional Note:* Celery aids in fighting kidney disease, arthritis, high blood pressure and diabetes. Dill has antioxidant and anti-bacterial properties.

## Radish and Apple Salsa

1 cup radishes, diced
1 cup apple, diced

1 cup peanuts, raw
½ cup red onions, minced
½ cup parsley, minced
1 T flaxseed oil
1 T organic apple cider
¼ t sea salt

Mix radishes apples, peanuts, parsley and onions. Stir thoroughly. Stir in seasonings. Pour flaxseed oil and apple cider. Stir thoroughly and adjust seasonings to taste.

***Nutritional note:*** *Radishes are high in potassium. They aid in fighting obesity and help dissolve gallstones. They are beneficial for the teeth, gums, nerves, hair and nails. Apples aid in liver health and help to prevent the formation of kidney stones. Peanuts are high in potassium and help to fight high blood pressure.*

## Black-eyed Pea Salsa

2 cups black-eyed peas
1 cup whole kernel corn
1 cup tomatoes, diced
2 T cilantro, minced
½ cup red bell pepper, minced
½ cup red onion, minced
2 T olive oil
2 T lemon juice
1 T garlic powder
1 t black pepper
½ t cayenne pepper
¼ t sea salt

Mix black-eyed peas, corn and tomatoes. Stir thoroughly. Blend in cilantro, red bell pepper and onion. Stir thoroughly. Add seasonings. Stir thoroughly. Pour in olive oil and lime juice. Stir thoroughly.

**Nutritional Note:** *Black-eyed peas are high in potassium, iron, protein and fiber. Red bell pepper is an excellent source of vitamin C and potassium.*

## Green peas and Corn Salsa

2 cups green peas
2 cups whole corn kernels
2 cups tomatoes, diced
½ cup red bell peppers, diced
1 cup scallions, minced
2 T fresh oregano, minced or dried flakes
½ cup parsley, minced
2 T flaxseed oil
1 T lemon juice
2 T garlic powder
1 t cayenne pepper
½ t sea salt

Combine green peas, corn and tomatoes. Stir thoroughly. Add in red peppers, scallions, oregano and parsley. Stir thoroughly. Stir in garlic powder, cayenne pepper and sea salt. Add flaxseed oil and lemon juice. Stir thoroughly.

**Nutritional note:** *Green peas are beneficial to heart and bone health. They are very high in Vitamin K. Oregano has antioxidant and disease preventing properties.*

## Pineapple Salsa

2 cups pineapple, diced
2 T cilantro, minced
2 T red onion, minced
2 T red bell pepper, diced
½ cup macadamia nuts, chopped
2 T ginger juice

1 T lemon juice
2 T garlic powder
¼ t salt
1 t honey (optional)

Blend pineapple, cilantro, red onion, red bell pepper and macadamia nuts. Add in garlic powder and salt. Stir thoroughly. Blend in lemon juice, ginger juice and honey. Stir thoroughly.

*Nutritional note: Pineapple contains papain which aids in digestion. Pineapple also aids in combating obesity, high blood pressure, arthritis and tumors. Macadamia nuts promote heart health and aid in combating anemia.*

## Pear and Ginger Salsa

2 cups pears, diced
1 t lemon zest
2 T parsley, minced
½ cup walnuts, chopped
¼ cup cilantro, minced
2 T yellow pepper, minced
1 T ginger juice
½ t honey

Combine pears, lemon zest, parsley, walnuts, cilantro and yellow pepper. Stir thoroughly. Add ginger juice and honey. Stir thoroughly.

*Nutritional note: Pears aid in digestion, high blood pressure, obesity, poor complexion and inflamed colon. Ginger has anti-inflammatory properties and boosts the immune system.*

## Papaya and Cantaloupe Salsa

1 cup papaya, diced
1 cantaloupe, diced

2 T parsley, minced
2 T red pepper, diced
2 T red onion, minced
½ cup pecans, chopped
1 T ground cinnamon
½ t cayenne pepper
Pinch of salt

Combine papaya, cantaloupe, pepper, parsley, onions and pecans. Stir thoroughly. Add cinnamon, cayenne pepper and salt. Stir thoroughly.

**Nutritional note:** *Papaya is high in potassium. It is also high in papain which aids in digestion. Cantaloupe is high in Vitamin A and potassium. It aids in fighting high blood pressure, obesity, arthritis, skin diseases, blood deficiencies and disorders of the kidney and bladder.*

# Salads

The majority of these salads are designed for you to enjoy your fruits, vegetables, nuts, seeds and herbs in their most natural state. Each salad includes such a variety of ingredients so that the salad itself can be your meal, especially if you are a vegetarian. If you are not, one of the best ways to eat these salads is along with your favorite grilled or roasted meat.

You do not need salad dressings with these salads. Most of the recipes call for an oil, lemon juice, another fruit juice and seasonings. You will reduce the amount of calories using this method instead of adding salad dressings. Season your salads up with your favorite spices!

*This is one of the easiest, healthiest and tastiest salads that there is! While I am giving you a good combination to work with, you can add whatever vegetables, nuts or other ingredients that you would like to customize this salad into your own.*

## Garlic Olive Salad

4 cups kale, chopped
2 cups red cabbage, chopped
2 cups lettuce, chopped
1 cup tomatoes, diced
1 cup cucumbers, diced
½ cup cilantro, minced
½ cup red onion, minced
½ cup red bell pepper, diced
2 T olive oil
2 T garlic powder

½ t sea salt
2 T olive tapenade—optional
10 peperoncinis—optional

Chop the kale, red cabbage and lettuce into ½ inch squares. Mix kale, red cabbage, lettuce, tomatoes, cucumbers cilantro, red onion and red bell pepper in a large bowl. Add olive oil. Stir ingredients together until oil is distributed evenly throughout the salad. Add garlic powder and sea salt. Stir until evenly distributed. Decorate with peperoncinis and tapenade.

You may add avocado, pecans or whatever nuts you prefer. You may also add pears, apples or whatever fruit of your choice.

***Nutritional note:*** *Cabbage is a cruciferous vegetable which has been proven to fight cancer. The red cabbage has significantly more nutrients than the green cabbage, while they do possess mainly the same qualities. The cabbage helps to lower the bad cholesterol and is a blood cleanser. It promotes healthy teeth, gums, hair and nails. It is helpful in cases of obesity, diabetes, iron deficiency and kidney and bladder disorders.*

## Pomegranate Salad

2 cups red cabbage, chopped
2 cups kale, chopped
1 cup iceberg lettuce, chopped
1 cup cucumber, diced*
½ cup cilantro, minced*
¼ cup red onion, minced*
1 cup carrots, finely minced
½ cup pecans, pieces
½ cup pomegranate seeds
2 T olive oil
2 T pomegranate juice
½ cup apple cider
1 t lemon juice
½ t sea salt

Mix cabbage, kale, lettuce, cilantro and red onion together. Stir in olive oil, lemon juice, apple cider and salt. Stir thoroughly. Layer remaining ingredients on top of mixture for beautiful presentation in this order: cucumber, carrots, pecans, pomegranate seeds.

*You may use the cucumber salsa instead of preparing this item individually.

**Nutritional note:** *The pomegranate is a blood purifier. It relieves liver congestion and helps to fight obesity, arthritis and obesity. It helps to prevent the formation of unwanted blood clots. Pomegranate juice is a powerful antioxidant and has anti-aging qualities. It is beneficial to cardio vascular health. Tests have proven that it helps to fight prostate cancer.*

## Collard Greens Salad

2 cups collard greens, chopped
1 cup cauliflower, chopped
2 cups lettuce, chopped
1 cup cucumbers, dice
½ cup cilantro, minced
½ cup red onion, finely chopped
1 cup avocado, chopped
1 cup pears
1 cup walnuts
2 T olive oil
3 T apple cider
1 t lemon juice
Pinch of salt

Mix collard greens, cauliflower, lettuce, cucumbers, cilantro and onion. Stir thoroughly. Add olive oil, apple cider, lemon juice and salt. Stir thoroughly. Garnish with avocados, pears and walnuts.

Collard greens can be eaten without ham hocks and bacon! This salad is so refreshing and filling!

**Nutritional note:** *Collards promote colon health. They are high in Vitamin A, Vitamin C and calcium. They are helpful in cases of anemia, liver trouble, constipation, arthritis and obesity. Cauliflower is a cruciferous vegetable with cancer fighting qualities. It is s blood purifier. It aids in cases of anemia, high blood pressure and kidney and bladder disorders.*

## Blueberry Salad

3 cups kale, chopped
1 cup lettuce, chopped
½ cup red bell pepper, diced
½ cup tomatoes, chopped
1 cup avocado, chopped
½ cup celery, diced
2 T red onions, minced
1 cup blueberries
1 cup pecans, chopped
2 T flax seed oil
1 T honey
1 t cinnamon
1 t lemon juice
½ t cayenne pepper
½ t garlic powder
Pinch of sea salt

Mix kale, lettuce, red bell pepper, tomatoes, avocado, celery, onion, blueberries and pecans. Stir thoroughly. Pour in oil and honey. Stir thoroughly. Add cayenne pepper, garlic powder and salt. Stir thoroughly.

**Nutritional note:** *Avocados are high in potassium which makes them beneficial in cases of high blood pressure. Studies have proven them helpful in cases of oral, breast and prostate cancers. Blueberries are blood cleansers. They are helpful in cases of anemia, obesity, diarrhea, menstrual disorders and poor skin complexion.*

## Strawberry Salad

1 cup beet greens or chard, chopped
2 cups kale, chopped
2 cups lettuce, chopped
1 cup cucumber, cubed
¼ cup cilantro, minced
¼ cup red onion, minced
¼ cup beets, finely chopped
¼ cup carrots, finely chopped
1 T red bell pepper, minced
1 T almonds, chopped or sliced
¼ cup strawberries
1 T lemon juice
½ cup pomegranate juice
2 T olive oil
2 T garlic powder
1 T dried basil
Pinch of sea salt

Mix beet greens, kale, lettuce, cucumber, cilantro and onion together. Pour in lemon juice, pomegranate juice and olive oil. Add garlic powder, dried basil and salt. Mix thoroughly. Mix beets, carrots and red bell pepper together. Put mixture on top of salad. Layer the strawberries on top. Top off salad with almonds.

This is a very healthy and beautiful salad. This is a great and tasty way to eat beets!

***Nutritional note:*** *Beet greens are a great source of Vitamin A, calcium and potassium. They have been reported to aid in cases of obesity, anemia, constipation, skin disorders, gas, gout, tumors and tuberculosis. Beets are blood builders and are excellent for the red blood corpuscles. They are recommended for kidney and bladder ailments, skin disorders, anemia and menstrual problems. Strawberries are a skin-cleansing food. They help to rid the blood of toxins. They are recommended for gout, high blood pressure and skin cancer.*

## Turnip Greens and Spinach Salad

1 cup turnip greens, chopped
1 cup spinach, chopped
1 cup lettuce, chopped
1 cup cucumbers, diced
1 cup parsley, minced
½ cup red onion, minced
½ cup beets, finely diced
1 cup carrots, finely diced
1 cup grapefruit bits
1 cup raisins
1 cup sunflower seeds
2 T olive oil
2 T pomegranate juice
1 t lemon juice
1 T garlic powder
1 t ground cinnamon
Pinch of salt

Mix turnip greens (you may also use mustard in place of the turnip greens), spinach, lettuce, cucumbers, parsley, and onion. Add olive oil, pomegranate juice and lemon juice. Stir thoroughly. Add garlic powder, ground cinnamon and salt. Stir thoroughly. Mix beets, carrots, and sunflower seeds together separately. Add to the top of the salad. Layer the salad with the grapefruit bits. Top the salad with raisins.

***Nutritional note:*** *Turnip greens are high in Vitamin A. They are helpful in cases of anemia, high blood pressure, obesity, bladder disorders, poor complexion, arthritis, gout and toxemia. Raisins are high in potassium. They have strength building qualities and are helpful in fighting low blood pressure.*

## Sweet Potato Salad

2 cups kale (green or red), chopped

2 cups lettuce, chopped
2 cups sweet potato, cubed
1 cup cucumbers, cubed
¼ cup cilantro, minced
¼ cup red onions, minced
1 cup carrots, finely minced
1 cup pecans, chopped
1 cup fuji apples, cubed
2 T flaxseed oil
1 T pomegranate juice
1 t lemon juice
1 T ground cinnamon
2 T garlic powder
Dash of salt

Mix kale, lettuce, cucumbers, cilantro and onions. Stir thoroughly. Add pomegranate juice, lemon juice and flaxseed oil. Stir thoroughly. Add garlic powder, cinnamon and salt. Stir thoroughly. Mix sweet potatoes and apples together separately. Add mixture to the top of salad. Mix carrots and pecans. Layer the mixture on top of the salad.

**Nutritional note:** *Sweet potatoes are rich in beta carotene. They have anti-oxidant and anti-inflammatory properties. Flaxseed oil is reported to support heart health and helps with annoying complications from menopause.*

## Collard Green and Broccoli

2 cups collard greens, chopped
1 cup broccoli, chopped
2 cups lettuce, chopped
2 cups cauliflower, chopped
1 cup of tomatoes, cubed
1 cup cucumber, diced
¼ cup red onion, minced
½ cup carrots, finely minced
1 cup apples, cubed

1 cup peanuts, raw
2 T olive oil
½ cup organic apple cider
1 t lemon juice
Pinch of salt

Mix collard greens, broccoli, lettuce, cauliflower, tomatoes, cucumber and red onion. Mix thoroughly. Add olive oil, cider, lemon juice and salt. Stir thoroughly. Add carrots to the top of salad. Mix apples and peanuts together and layer on top of the salad.

*Nutritional note: This salad has been specifically designed to be beneficial for your hair. Broccoli is a good source of Vitamin A, calcium and potassium. This is a cruciferous vegetable which has been reported to prevent cancer. It is an excellent food to fight obesity, toxemia, constipation and high blood pressure. Lettuce does have nutritional value! It has been found to be helpful in cases of anemia, constipation, obesity, circulatory diseases, urinary tract diseases and arthritis. Of course, the richer the color of the lettuce, the more nutritional value it provides.*

## Spinach and Black Bean Salad

2 cups spinach, chopped
2 cups turnip greens, chopped
2 cups lettuce, chopped
1 cup black beans, cooked and drained
¼ cup red onion, minced
1 cup roma tomatoes, diced
2 T parsley, minced
1 cup raisins
1 dried cranberries
½ cup sesame seeds
1 cup walnuts, chopped
2 T flaxseed oil
3 T apple cider
1 t lemon juice
Pinch of salt

Mix spinach, turnip greens, lettuce, black beans, onion, tomatoes and parsley. Stir thoroughly. Add flaxseed oil, apple cider, lemon juice and pinch of salt and stir thoroughly. Mix raisins, cranberries, sesame seeds and walnuts together and layer on top.

***Nutritional note:*** *This salad has been specifically designed to be beneficial to the liver. Turnip greens are high in Vitamin A and calcium. They are an excellent food for people suffering from anemia, obesity, high blood pressure, asthma, liver ailments, gout and bladder ailments. They also help with skin complexion and purifying the blood. Sesame seeds are high in potassium. They are a good source of Vitamin E which makes them good for the heart and nerves. They can be instrumental in removing worms from the intestinal tract.*

## Tuna Salad

1 cup tuna mix
3 cups iceberg lettuce, chopped
¼ cup cucumbers, diced
1 T cilantro, minced
1 T red onion, minced
1 T tomato, diced
1 T avocado, chopped
1 T olive tapenade
2 peperoncinis
Dash Cajun seasoning (Zatarains or Tony Chachere's)
1 t lemon juice
1 T olive oil

Put lettuce in salad bowl. Mix cucumber, cilantro, onion, olive and lemon juice together and layer on top of the salad. Scoop tuna mix and place in the middle of the salad. Decorate salad with the remaining ingredients. Mix tomatoes and avocado and circle around tuna. Sprinkle the tapenade on top of the salad. Put peperoncinis on top. Sprinkle the Cajun seasoning on top on the tuna.

## Tuna Mix—Mayo Version

1 8 oz. can tuna
2 T mayonnaise
½ teaspoon garlic powder
Dash sea salt
½ teaspoon black pepper

Thoroughly mix all ingredients together. Add more mayonnaise, if tuna is too dry.

## Tuna—Yogurt Version

1 8 oz. can tuna
1 teaspoon plain yogurt
1 t mustard
½ t garlic powder
½ t onion powder
½ t black pepper
Pinch sea salt

Thoroughly mix all ingredients together. Add more yogurt and mustard, if tuna is too dry.

## Chicken Salad Version

1 can of chicken, drained
1 T mayonnaise
1 T mustard
½ t garlic powder
½ t onion powder
Pinch of sea salt

Thoroughly mix all ingredients together. Add more mayonnaise and mustard, if chicken is too dry.

*Nutritional note:* Lettuce contains a considerable amount of Vitamin E and potassium which makes it valuable to heart health. Tomatoes contain Vitamin K which helps to prevent hemorrhaging.

## Spinach and Fuji Apple Salad

2 cups romaine lettuce, chopped
1 cup spinach, chopped
1 cup roma tomatoes, diced
1 cup artichoke hearts, diced
1 cup fuji apples, diced
1 cup black olives, chopped
½ cup red onions, thinly sliced
1 cup walnuts, chopped
1 cup feta cheese
2 T olive oil
1 t lemon juice

Chop lettuce and spinach into ¼ squares. Mix all ingredients together and stir thoroughly.

*Nutritional note:* Walnuts are a great source protein, phosphorus and potassium. It is good for constipation and improves metabolism.

## Mustard Greens and Pear Salad

2 cups romaine lettuce, chopped
2 cups mustard greens, chopped
1 cup avocado, diced
1 cup tomatoes, diced
½ cup capers
½ cup red onions, thinly sliced
1 cup sunflower seeds
1 cup pears, cubed
¼ cup parsley, minced
2 T olive oil

1 t lemon juice

Chop lettuce and greens into ½ inch squares. Mix all ingredients together and stir thoroughly.

*Nutritional note: Mustard greens are a great source of Vitamin A, Vitamin C and iron. Sunflower seeds are an excellent source of iron. They are said to nourish the entire body. They strengthen weak eyes, fingernails and teeth.*

## Pineapple Spinach Salad

6 cups baby spinach, chopped
2 cup pineapple, diced
2 cups carrot, shredded
1 cup raisins
1 cup cashews
1 cup cilantro
½ cup red onions, thinly sliced
2 T flaxseed oil
3 T apple cider
1 t lemon juice

Chop lettuce and spinach into ½ inch squares. Mix all ingredients together thoroughly. For variety you may add feta cheese with whatever choice of meat.

*Nutritional note: Cashews are valuable for heart health. It is recommended that we have at least 7 cashews per day. The fat in cashews is the same fat that our hearts are made of. They are also recommended for problems with teeth and gums.*

## Avocado and Walnut Salad

3 cups romaine lettuce, chopped
1 cup tomatoes, diced

1 cup avocado, diced
1 cup artichoke, diced
1 cup kalamata olives, diced
1 cup walnuts, chopped
½ cup red onion, thinly sliced
½ cup parmesan cheese, shaved
1 cup pears, cubed
2 T olive oil
1 t black pepper
1 t garlic powder

Chop lettuce and spinach into ½ inch squares. Mix all ingredients together. Stir thoroughly.

**Nutritional note:** *Artichokes are a natural diuretic and have proven effective in fighting liver ailments.*

# Entrées

Be sure to refer to the Nutritional Guide for information on the smoke points for oils. To ensure that you are preparing your meals to gain the highest possible nutritional benefits, make sure that you are not exceeding the smoke points for the oils that you are using. If you exceed the smoke point on certain oils, they will become toxic instead of beneficial to your health.

## *Orange Turmeric Chicken*

2 lbs of boneless skinless chicken
1 cup onions, chopped
2 T garlic, minced (or powder)
½ cup basil flakes (or fresh)
2 T ground turmeric
½ t cayenne pepper
½ t sea salt
½ cup orange juice
½ cup orange zest
2 T olive oil

Sauté onion in olive oil until tender. Add chicken. Cook chicken until it is white on all sides. Add more oil, if needed. Stir in minced garlic. Pour in orange juice. Add basil, turmeric, cayenne pepper and sea salt. Turn heat to low. Cover and simmer for 20 minutes or until done. Add orange zest when ready to serve.

## Orange Turmeric Shrimp

3 lbs shrimp, peeled and deveined
(use all of the same ingredients as above)


## Orange Turmeric Tofu

2 lbs Tofu, firm and squarely chopped
(use all of the same ingredients as above)

***Nutritional note:*** *Turmeric is reported to be a cleanser for the whole body. Studies have shown that it is helpful in cases of Alzheimer's disease, cancer, liver problems and arthritis. Turmeric has antioxidant, anti-inflammatory and anti-bacterial properties. It has heart protecting qualities. Basil is high in Vitamin K. It also has antioxidant, anti-inflammatory and anti-bacterial properties. The vitamins and nutrients in basil promote heart health by reducing the risk of stroke and prompting the muscles and blood vessels to relax.*


## Artichoke Mushroom Sauce

2 cups mushrooms, chopped
2 cups artichokes, chopped
1 medium onion, chopped
1 medium green bell pepper
24 oz. tomato sauce
2 T olive oil
3 T garlic powder
2 T oregano
2 T basil flakes
½ t sea salt
1 t black pepper
½ cup parmesan cheese (optional)

Sauté onions until they began to caramelize. Add bell pepper and sauté' together until the pepper is limp. Add mushrooms and sauté until tender. Add more oil if necessary to avoid sticking and burning. Stir in artichokes. Add tomato sauce. Continue to stir to avoid sticking. Add garlic powder, oregano, basil, sea salt and pepper. Add parmesan cheese, if desired. Reduce heat to low and let simmer for 15 minutes. Serve with pasta of your choice.

Other options:
Add 2 lbs of any meat of your choice such as:
Shrimp
Salmon
Crab meat
Chicken—Boneless skinless chicken breasts or thigh meat
Ground Chicken
Ground Turkey
Ground Beef
Sirloin Steak
Italian Sausage

Cook meat separately in olive oil until done. Drain and add to mixture right after you have sautéed the mushrooms. Cook the meat until it is done and finish the rest of the recipe as directed.

***Nutritional note:*** *Mushrooms are a good source of Vitamin B, Vitamin D, selenium and potassium. Studies have proven them helpful in fighting cancer and heart disease. Oregano is a good source of Vitamin K. It has anti-bacterial and antioxidant qualities.*

## Pan Fried Salmon

1 side of salmon
1 cup onion, chopped
2 T garlic, sliced
1 cup mushrooms, sliced
2 T olive oil
1 t black pepper
Pinch of salt

Other options—2 lbs of any of the meat below:
Chicken breasts
Boneless Skinless Chicken Thighs
Steak of your choice
Pork chops

Season salmon on both sides and set aside. Sauté onion, garlic and mushrooms until the onion is caramelized and the mushrooms are tender. Add more oil, if needed. Add salmon. Cover and cook on medium to low heat for 20 minutes or until salmon is done.

*Nutritional Note: Onion is good for high blood pressure. It is a natural diuretic. Salmon is one of the best fish to eat. It is a great source of Vitamin B12, Protein and Omega-3-fatty acid.*

## Cinnamon Chicken

2 lbs boneless skinless chicken thighs, cut into pieces
1 medium onion, diced
½ cup red pepper, diced
2 T olive oil
2 T balsamic vinegar
1 T cinnamon
½ t cayenne pepper
Pinch of sea salt

Sauté onion in olive oil until caramelized. Add red bell pepper and cook until limp. Stir in balsamic vinegar. Add in chicken. Season with cinnamon, cayenne pepper and salt and stir thoroughly. Bring to a boil. Then simmer for 30 minutes or until chicken is completely done.

*Nutritional Note: Cinnamon has proven to be helpful in cases Type 2 Diabetes and heart disease. It is also said to help lower bad cholesterol. Honey is a blood cleanser. It has anti-bacterial and antioxidant properties.*

## Pineapple Chicken

2 lbs boneless skinless chicken breasts
1 cup pineapple, cubed or crushed
½ cup pineapple juice
1 cup yellow onion, diced
1 cup cilantro, minced
2 T olive oil
1 T black pepper
Pinch of sea salt

Sauté onion in olive oil until caramelized. Add in chicken. Cook until chicken is white all over. Stir in cilantro. Stir in pineapple. Stir in pineapple juice. Add black pepper and salt. Bring to a boil. Simmer for about 30 minutes or until chicken is completely done.

*Nutritional note: Pineapple is good for high blood pressure. It is said to be helpful in cases of tumors. Chicken is a good source of protein, iron and niacin.*

## Salsa Chicken

2 lbs boneless skinless chicken thighs
1 medium jar of salsa (between 12-16 oz.)
1 cup onion, diced
½ cup cilantro
2 T olive oil

Sauté onion in olive oil until caramelized. Add in chicken and cook until chicken is white all over. Stir in cilantro. Stir in salsa. Bring to a boil. Simmer for about 30 minutes or until chicken is completely done.

*Nutritional note: Onions are high in potassium. They help to destroy worms and parasites in the body. Cilantro helps with digestion. It is high in Vitamin A and lutein. Lutein promotes eye health reducing the development of cataracts.*

## Baked Tilapia

6 filets of tilapia
2 T garlic powder
2 T onion powder
1 T Cajun seasoning
2 T olive oil

Wash tilapia thoroughly and pat dry. Cover all of the fillets with the olive oil. Sprinkle garlic powder, onion powder and Cajun seasoning onto each of the fillets. Bake for 20—30 minutes.

*Nutritional note: Tilapia is a great source of protein and iron. This is a fish that is low in fat which makes it excellent to eat when trying to lose weight.*

## Pepper Chicken

3 lbs boneless skinless chicken thighs, cut into small pieces
½ cup red bell pepper, diced
½ cup green bell pepper, diced
½ cup yellow bell pepper, diced
½ cup yellow onion, chopped
½ cup green onion, chopped
3 T olive oil
2 T garlic powder
2 T black pepper
Dash of salt
2 T balsamic vinegar

Sauté onion in 2 tablespoons of olive oil until caramelized. Add the remaining olive oil along with the red bell pepper, green bell pepper, yellow bell pepper and green onion. Cook until all of the vegetables are tender, stirring constantly. Add chicken. Continue to stir to make sure chicken does not burn. Cook chicken until it is white all over. Add more oil, if needed. Add garlic powder, black pepper and salt. Bring to a boil.

Then simmer fifteen minutes or until chicken is completely done. Serve over rice.

***Nutritional note:*** *Bell peppers are an excellent source of Vitamin C and potassium. They are helpful in maintaining the right alkaline balance in the body.*

## Basil Chicken

2 lbs boneless skinless chicken thighs or breasts
1 cup chopped fresh basil (or 3 T dried basil flakes)
1 cup green onion, chopped
2 T black pepper
2 T olive oil
Dash of salt

Sauté chicken in olive oil until chicken is white all over. Stir in green onion and basil. Add black pepper and salt. Bring to a boil and then simmer for about 15 minutes or until chicken is completely done.

***Nutritional note:*** *Basil is a great source of iron. It contains lutein which promotes heart health.*

## Tomato Gumbo

2 lbs boneless skinless chicken thighs, cut into small pieces
2 lbs prawns, peeled and deveined
2 kielbasa (beef, chicken, pork or turkey), sliced
4 cups fresh tomatoes, cubed
1 cup yellow onion, diced
1 cup green bell pepper, diced
1 cup red bell pepper, diced
½ cup celery, diced
½ cup parsley, minced
2 T garlic powder
1 t cayenne pepper

2 T Cajun seasoning
½ cup olive oil
1 cup of water
Dash of salt

*This gumbo does not have the flour and oil roux.*
Sauté onion in a large sauce pan or skillet until caramelized. Add red and green bell pepper, celery and parsley. Sauté until they are all tender. Add chicken and cook until done, stirring constantly to make sure that it does not burn. Stir in tomatoes. Add prawns and kielbasa. Stir in water. Add seasonings. Adjust to taste. Add more water if soup is too thick.

Serve over rice or pasta.

**Nutritional note:** *Tomatoes contain nicotinic acid which helps to reduce the bad cholesterol in the blood. They also contain Vitamin K which helps to prevent hemorrhaging.*


## Chris' After School Chicken and Rice Bake

10-12 pieces of chicken (drumsticks, thighs, breasts, wings or a combination)
2 cups of brown rice
3½ cups water
1 medium onion, diced
1 T black pepper
1 T Cajun seasoning
2 T garlic powder
1 T sage (optional)
½ t sea salt

Preheat oven at 400 degrees.
Pour brown rice and onion into 9" X 13" baking pan. Pour in water. Place the chicken in the pan. Add black pepper, garlic powder, Cajun seasoning and salt. Add sage, if desired. Stir ingredients to distribute the onion evenly throughout pan. Place chicken evenly throughout pan.

Add more seasonings to taste, if desired. Bake for 45 minutes or until chicken is done.

Other options: Add whatever vegetable you desire, such as corn, peas or green beans, ½ cup of water per cup of vegetable.

*Nutritional note: Brown rice is an excellent source of fiber and selenium. Studies have proven it to be helpful in maintaining good heart health.*

## Lemon Chicken

4 chicken breasts
½ cup yellow onion, diced
½ cup apple cider
½ cup lemon juice
1 T garlic powder
2 T basil flakes
¼ t sea salt

Preheat oven at 375 degrees.
Puncture chicken all over with a fork. Mix lemon juice and apple cider together. Place chicken in 9" X 13" baking pan. Slowly pour all over the chicken breasts. Leave juice in pan for the chicken to bake in. Season chicken with garlic powder, basil and salt. Bake for 30 minutes or until chicken is done.

Topping

½ cup lemon zest
1 T honey
2 T of apple cider and lemon juice mixture

Wash lemons thoroughly. You may need up to 3 lemons according to the size of the lemons to get ½ cup of zest. Grate the zest from the lemon rinds with a grater. Place lemon zest in a small mixing bowl. Add honey. Add apple cider and lemon juice mixture from the baked chicken. Stir ingredients together. Pour topping onto chicken when served. The remainder of the mixture may be used to serve over rice.

*Nutritional note: Lemons contain potent phytochemicals which make them effective as an antioxidant, free radical scavenger and immune system modulator. They also have anti-inflammatory properties. Lemons are a great source of Vitamin C. They help to fight colds and infections.*

## Balsamic Salmon

1 side of salmon
2 T garlic powder
2 T onion powder
2 T black pepper
1 cup balsamic vinegar salad dressing

Preheat oven at 375 degrees.
Season salmon on both sides with garlic powder, onion powder and black pepper. You may do this in the pan that you will bake the salmon in. Pour salad dressing evenly over the salmon. Bake for 30 minutes or until done.

*Nutritional note: Studies have shown that balsamic vinegar has been effective in fighting cancer, controlling diabetes and promoting heart health.*

## Spaghetti Squash
*(raw and meatless)*

1 large spaghetti squash
4 roma tomatoes, chopped
1 T garlic, minced
2 T parsley, minced
2 T basil, minced
1 T red onion, minced

2 T olive oil
1 t black pepper
¼ t sea salt

Spaghetti
Penetrate your knife about one inch into the squash. Run it all around the spaghetti squash. Open the squash and pour the spaghetti into a strainer. Rinse thoroughly. Gently pull the spaghetti apart with a fork. Pour spaghetti into a bowl. Stir olive oil into spaghetti thoroughly. Set spaghetti aside.

Sauce
Add tomatoes, garlic, parsley, basil, red onion, black pepper, salt together and mix thoroughly. Serve sauce on top of spaghetti.

**Nutritional note:** *Spaghetti squash is high in antioxidants. It is a good source of Vitamin A which boosts the immune system.*

## Pasta and Chicken

2 lbs. ground chicken
2 cups sundried tomatoes, chopped
½ cup yellow onion, diced
½ cup green bell pepper, diced
2 T garlic, fresh minced or powder
2 T basil, fresh minced or dried flakes
2 T oregano, fresh minced or dried flakes
4 T olive oil
1 t black pepper
½ t sea salt

Pasta
Prepare desired pasta as directed.

Sauce
Sauté onion in olive oil until caramelized. Add green bell pepper and sauté until the pepper is limp. Add meat and cook until meat is mostly

done. Stir in tomatoes and cook until tender. Add garlic, basil, oregano, pepper and salt and stir in thoroughly. Turn heat down to low and simmer for at least 15 minutes. Serve over pasta.

*Nutritional note: Sundried tomatoes contain lycopene which to fight cancer and cardiovascular disease.*


## Pasta Stir Fry

1 lb pasta
2 cups broccoli, chopped
2 cups mushrooms, chopped
2 cups carrots, sliced
1 cup green onions, diced
1 cup yellow onion, diced
2 T jalapeno, thinly sliced and seeded
2 T olive oil
2 T garlic powder
½ t sea salt

Pasta
Prepare pasta of choice as directed.

Vegetables
Sauté yellow onion in olive oil in a large sauce pan until caramelized. Add mushroom and sauté them until limp. Add more oil as needed. Stir in carrots, green onion and jalapeno. Let cook for about 3 minutes, stirring constantly. Add broccoli and stir thoroughly. Add garlic powder and salt. Stir thoroughly. Cover and remove from heat. Let it set for 5—10 minutes. Stir in pasta.

*Nutritional note: The nutrients in carrots help to promote colon health, reduce the risk of cancer and improve vision.*

## Summer Squash and Chicken Casserole

2 lbs boneless skinless chicken thighs, chopped
3 cups winter squash, chopped
1 cup yellow onion, diced
1 cup green onion, diced
1 cup celery, diced
2 eggs, medium
½ cup plain yogurt
2 T turmeric
2 T garlic powder
1 t sage, ground
1 t black pepper
¼ t sea salt

Preheat oven at 375 degrees.
Stir all ingredients together and pour into baking dish. Bake for 45 minutes or until chicken is done.

*Nutritional note: Summer squash is a great source of fiber. Studies have proven that it is good for prostate health. It has antioxidant and anti-inflammatory properties.*

## Tomato and Turmeric Pasta

2 lbs chicken, chopped
2 cups tomatoes, diced
1 cup onion, diced
1 cup green bell pepper, diced
1 cup parsley, minced
1 cup plain yogurt
2 cups water
2 T turmeric
2 T garlic powder or minced garlic
2 T olive oil
½ t cayenne
Pinch of sea salt

1 lb pasta
Prepare pasta of choice.

Sauté chicken and cook until white on all sides. Add parsley and stir thoroughly. Add tomatoes and cook until soft and mushy. Stir constantly to avoid burning. Add 1 cup of water and stir thoroughly. Stir in yogurt. Add garlic, cayenne pepper and salt. Stir thoroughly. Add remaining water. Bring to a boil. Then turn heat to low and let simmer for 10 minutes.

Other options instead of chicken:
Beef
Shrimp
Pork roast
Eggplant
Tofu
Cauliflower

**Nutritional note:** *Turmeric has been reported to be helpful in treating diabetes, arthritis and liver disorders.*

## *Jambalaya*

4 T canola oil
2 T whole wheat flour
1 lb boneless skinless chicken thighs, chopped
1 lb turkey kielbasa, sliced
1 lb shrimp, shelled, deveined, tail off
2 cups tomatoes, diced
1 cup yellow onion, diced
½ cup green onion, diced
½ cup red bell pepper, diced
½ cup green bell pepper, diced
½ cup celery, diced
2 T garlic powder
1 t Worcestershire sauce
1 t cayenne pepper

1 t salt
4 cups rice, cooked

In large pot stir flour in oil on medium heat until it is smooth and brown. Add yellow onion, green onion, red bell pepper, green bell pepper and celery. Stir thoroughly. Stir in tomatoes and let cook for 5 minutes, stirring constantly. Stir in chicken, continuing to stir. Add garlic powder, Worcestershire sauce, cayenne pepper and salt. Stir thoroughly. Add turkey sausage and shrimp. Turn heat down to low. Cover and let simmer for 10 minutes or until shrimp are pink. Cook rice separately and mix together when ready to serve.

**Nutritional note:** *Green onions (scallions) are anti-bacterial and anti-fungal. Scallions are helpful in cases of colon cancer by inhibiting cancer growth.*

## Cajun Chili

1 lb ground chicken
1 lb turkey kielbasa, sliced
2 lb crayfish tails or small shrimp
2 cups pinto beans, cooked
4 cups tomatoes, diced
1 cup yellow onion, diced
½ cup green onion, diced
1 cup green bell pepper, diced
1 cup red bell pepper, diced
4 T canola oil
3 T garlic powder
2 T chili powder
2 T cumin
1 t Worcestershire sauce
½ t cayenne pepper
½ t salt
2 cups water (if needed)

In a large pot, sauté yellow and green onion in 2 tablespoons of canola oil. Stir in green and red bell peppers with the remaining canola oil and sauté. Stir in chicken. Cook until most of the chicken is done. Add in tomatoes. Stir thoroughly and cook until tender. Add garlic powder, chili powder, cumin, Worcestershire sauce, cayenne pepper and salt. Stir thoroughly. Add turkey sausage, fish and pinto beans. Stir in thoroughly. Add seasonings. Stir thoroughly. Add water slowly and incrementally, if chili is too thick. Turn heat down to low. Cover and let simmer for at least 15 minutes. Make sure the shrimp pink and done before serving. Serve with rice or as a main dish with cornbread.

**Nutritional note:** *Cumin is a good source of iron. Studies have proven that it has cancer preventing qualities.*

## Spicy Roasted Chicken

1 whole chicken
½ cup apple cider vinegar
2 T honey
2 T garlic powder
2 T onion powder
1 T water
1 T black pepper
¼ t cayenne pepper
½ t sea salt
2 T olive oil

Preheat oven at 400 degrees.
Remove extra parts from inside the chicken. Thoroughly wash chicken inside and out. Place chicken in roasting pan. Pierce chicken with a fork all over. Mix all of the seasonings, water and olive oil together. Pour mixture all over the chicken slowly. Cover and cook chicken for 20 minutes. Remove chicken from oven. Dip the mixture from pan and pour over chicken again. Cook for another 20 minutes or until done uncovered.

*Greta Andrews*

**Nutritional note:** *Apple cider vinegar is a strengthener of the immune system. It helps to prevent the formation of gall bladder stones and it helps to fight infections in the urinary tract.*

# Soups and Sides

While it is best to eat our vegetables and fruits in their rawest state, cooking them can sometimes have their advantages. Some are more digestible and have more fiber when they are cooked. Do be mindful of the smoke points for the oils that you use when cooking. If the oil exceeds its smoke point, it can become toxic.

## *Kale*

4 cups kale chopped
1 cup onion, chopped
2 T garlic, minced
2 T olive oil
Pinch of sea salt

Sauté onion in olive oil in skillet until caramelized. Stir in garlic. Stir in kale. Add salt. Stir thoroughly. Cover and turn off heat.

You can use this same basic recipe for many other vegetables such as those listed below:
Collards, turnips, cabbage, mustard greens, turnip greens, green beans, broccoli, cauliflower, asparagus and squash.

You may also use this same recipe and bake the ingredients instead of stir frying. You may also use onion powder in place of the raw onions when baking.

*Nutritional note: This cruciferous vegetable is one of the healthiest side dishes to can prepare. It is loaded with antioxidants and cancer fighting nutrients. It is off the charts in Vitamin K with high contents of Vitamin A and calcium.*

## Spinach

4 cups raw spinach
1 T garlic, minced
1 T olive oil
Pinch of sea salt
½ t lemon juice

Sauté garlic in olive oil in sauce pan. Turn heat off. Stir in spinach. Add salt and lemon juice. Cover and remove from heat. Let it set for five to ten minutes.

Other options: Kale, mustard greens.

**Nutritional note:** *Spinach is a powerful vegetable that you can never eat enough of. It is also loaded with Vitamin K, Vitamin A, potassium and the list goes on! Whether cooked or raw, we should include spinach in our diets on a regular basis.*

## Zesty Okra

4 cups of okra, chopped
1 cup onion, diced
2 T olive oil
2 T minced garlic (or powder)
2 T basil (dried flakes or fresh)
2 cups of salsa
1 t black pepper
1 t Cajun seasoning (Zatarains or Tony Chachere's)
Dash of salt

Sauté onion in olive oil in large sauce pan or pot until caramelized. Stir in okra. Pour in salsa. Stir thoroughly. Add garlic, basil, black pepper,

Cajun seasoning and salt. Stir thoroughly. Bring to a boil. Then cover and simmer for about 15 minutes or the okra is as tender or desired. Add water, if desired.

You may prepare this as a vegetarian dish with the directions above or you may add whatever meat you would like such as: chicken, kielbasa of any type, ground beef, beef stew meat, pork loin and shrimp.

*Nutritional note: Okra is a good source of potassium. It has been found to be helpful in cases of stomach ulcers and inflammation of the lungs and colon.*

## Chicken Noodle Soup

1 whole chicken or 12 pieces of chicken, such as legs or thighs
1 package of angel hair pasta, cooked
2 cups potatoes, cubed
1 package mixed vegetables
1 cup celery, diced
1 cup green bell pepper, diced
1 cup onion, diced
2 cups carrots, sliced
1 cup parsley, minced
1 cup green onions, chopped
3 T garlic powder
1 T Cajun seasoning
2 T black pepper
1 t sea salt
3 T olive oil

Sauté onion in 2 tablespoons of olive oil in large pot until caramelized. Add remaining olive oil and green bell pepper, celery, green onions and parsley. Sauté until all vegetables are limp. Add four cup of water. Add potatoes, carrots and chicken. Add more water if needed to cover all ingredients. Cook ingredients for minutes. Stir in mixed vegetables. Add more water, if needed. Add garlic powder, Cajun seasoning, black pepper and salt. Stir thoroughly. Bring to a boil. Then let simmer until chicken is done and potatoes and carrots are soft.

**Nutritional note:** *Even in powder form, garlic is still powerful in its health and healing qualities. It promotes heart health by helping to reduce high blood pressure and lowering bad cholesterol. Studies suggest that it improve our iron metabolism.*

## Salsa Beans

4 cups of black beans (or beans of choice)
2 cups water
2 cups tomato salsa of choice
2 T minced garlic (or garlic powder)
1 cup yellow onions, chopped
1 cup of green bell pepper, chopped
½ cup red bell pepper, minced
2 T olive oil
1 T cumin
1 T chili powder
1 t sea salt
½ t cayenne pepper

Soak beans overnight or for 8 hours. Sauté onion and pepper in olive oil. After the vegetables have caramelized, add meat, if desired, and cook until done. Then add water. Bring to a boil. Add beans. Add more water, enough to cover all ingredients. Add seasonings, cumin, chili powder, sea salt and cayenne pepper. Cover and let simmer for 2 hours or until all beans are as soft as you desire. Add more seasonings to taste.

You may add any of the meat choices below:
Kielbasa—turkey, beef or pork
Ground beef, turkey or chicken
Beef stew meat
Boneless skinless chicken breasts
Boneless skinless chicken thighs

Pork—ham, pork roast or bacon

***Nutritional note:*** *Black beans are high in antioxidants. They promote heart health. Black beans are one of the best sources of iron, fiber and protein.*

## Collard Greens

4 bunches of collard greens, chopped
1 medium onion, diced
2 roma tomatoes, chopped
4 sliced garlic cloves (or 2 T garlic powder)
1 t apple cider vinegar
½ t Cajun seasoning
2 T olive oil
Pinch of sea salt

Sauté onion in olive oil in sauce pan or skillet until caramelized. Stir in sliced garlic. Stir in tomatoes and cook them for approximately 3 minutes, stirring constantly. Add collard greens. Stir collards until they are all moist from the sauce in the pan. Stir in vinegar. Add salt and Cajun seasoning. Stir thoroughly. Bring to boil, then turn heat down to low. Let simmer for about 15 minutes or until collards are as tender as desired.

***Nutritional note:*** *Collard greens help to lower bad cholesterol. Studies have shown that eating this cruciferous vegetable will cause colon cancer cells to commit suicide!*

## Vegetable Soup

2 cups green beans
2 cups corn
2 cups green peas
2 cups potatoes, cubed
3 cups tomatoes, diced

2 cups carrots
2 cups yellow onion, diced
1 cup green bell pepper
1 cup red bell pepper
2 T olive oil
2 T garlic powder
2 T basil flakes
1 T black pepper
1 t sea salt
Water

Sauté onion in 2 tablespoons of the olive oil until caramelized. Add green and red bell peppers and sauté until they are limp. Add more oil, if needed, to sauté the peppers. Add tomatoes and cook for 5 minutes, stirring thoroughly. Add 2 cups of water; then add potatoes and carrots. Cook on medium heat for 20 minutes. Add green beans, corn and peas. Add more water, if needed, enough to cover all vegetables. Stir thoroughly. Add garlic powder, basil, pepper and salt. Add more seasoning, if desired, to taste.

**Nutritional note:** *Green beans have anti-inflammatory and antioxidant qualities. Surprisingly, they are a good source of omega-3 fatty acids.*

## Chicken Tomato Soup

Use same recipe as above.
4 cups boneless skinless chicken breasts or thighs, cubed

Add chicken to onions and peppers. Cook until white on all sides. Add more water, if needed. Follow the rest of the recipe as instructed above.

## Creamy Garlic Potatoes

4 cups potatoes
3 T plain yogurt

1 T garlic powder
½ t sea salt
Dash of black pepper
5 cups water

Pour water into pot and bring to boil. Add potatoes and cook on high heat for 30 minutes or until all potatoes are tender. Drain water from potatoes using a colander. Pour potatoes into mixing bowl. Stir in yogurt, garlic powder and sea salt. Using a fork, whip potato mixture until creamy. Sprinkle black pepper on top of potatoes.

*Nutritional note: Eating potatoes in a healthy way can contribute to good health. They are a great source of Vitamin B6, Vitamin C and fiber.*

## Herbal Brown Rice

2 cups brown rice
2 cup of water
2 cups vegetable broth
½ cup green onion, chopped
½ cup parsley, minced
½ t sea salt
½ t black pepper

Pour water and broth into pot and bring to a boil. Add in rice and bring to back to a boil. Turn heat down to simmer and cover. Simmer for about 30 minutes or until rice is tender. When rice is done, pour into serving bowl. Add onion, parsley, salt and pepper. Stir thoroughly and serve.

*Nutritional note: Brown rice is a great source of protein, Iron, phosphorus, potassium and fiber.*

## Beef Stew

4 cups beef stew meat
3 cups tomatoes, diced
2 cups potatoes, cubed
2 cups carrots, chopped
2 cups green beans
1 cup yellow onions, minced
1 cup green bell pepper, minced
1 bay leaf
2 T garlic powder
2 T basil flakes
1 t Worcestershire sauce
2 T olive oil
1 t black pepper
1 t sea salt
Water

Sauté onions in oil in pot until tender. Add green bell pepper and cook until tender. Add stew meat and cook until brown on all sides. Add 3 cups of water. Then add potatoes and carrots. Add more water, if needed, to cover all ingredients. Cook on medium heat for 10 minutes. Add green beans, bay leaf, garlic powder, basil, Worcestershire sauce, black pepper and salt. Stir thoroughly. Turn heat to low to simmer. Simmer for 15 minutes or until potatoes and carrots are tender.

*Nutritional note: Bay leaves are high in Vitamin A, Vitamin C, iron and potassium. Their rich flavor adds to any stew or tomato based dish.*

## Cauliflower and Broccoli Soup

2 cups cauliflower, chopped
2 cups broccoli, chopped
2 cups roma tomatoes, wedged
1 cup yellow onions, diced
½ cup garlic, minced
1 cup vegetable broth

2 T olive oil
½ cup plain yogurt
2 T turmeric
1 t black pepper
1 t sea salt
Water

Sauté onion in oil in a large pot until tender. Add garlic and sauté until limp. Add tomatoes and sauté until soft and they began to get mushy. Add 1 cup of water and then cauliflower. Stir thoroughly. Add broth and broccoli and stir thoroughly. Add yogurt, turmeric, black pepper and sea salt. Stir thoroughly. Turn heat to low, cover and simmer for 10 minutes.

*Nutritional note: Broccoli and cauliflower are two of the most powerful vegetables there are. Together you get the benefit of their anti-inflammatory and antioxidant properties. They have been reported to fight bladder, prostate, colon, breast and ovarian cancers.*

## Turmeric Chicken Soup

4 chicken breasts, cubed
2 cups cauliflower, chopped
2 cups tomatoes, diced
1 cup corn
1 cup potatoes, cubed
1 cup onion, diced
1 cup green bell pepper, diced
3 T olive oil
1 cup plain yogurt
3 cup water
2 T turmeric
2 T garlic powder
½ t cayenne pepper
1 t sea salt
1 t black pepper

Sauté onions in oil in pot until tender. Add green bell pepper and sauté until tender. Add chicken and cook for few minutes until all sides of meat is white. Add tomatoes and cook until soft and mushy. Pour in water. Add potatoes and cook for 10 minutes. Add cauliflower and cook for 10 minutes. Add corn, garlic powder, turmeric, sea salt and pepper. Add yogurt and stir in thoroughly. Turn heat down and simmer for 15 minutes.

***Nutritional note:*** *Plain yogurt is a great source of Vitamin B12, calcium and protein. It can be used in the place of regular milk and butter.*

## Tomato and Turmeric Soup

2 lbs chicken, chopped
2 cups tomatoes, diced
1 cup onion, diced
1 cup green bell pepper, diced
1 cup parsley, minced
1 cup plain yogurt
2 cups water
2 T turmeric
2 T garlic powder or minced garlic
2 T olive oil
½ t cayenne
Pinch of sea salt

Sauté onion in olive oil until caramelized. Add green bell pepper and cook until tender. Add chicken and cook until white on all sides. Add parsley and stir thoroughly. Add tomatoes and cook until soft and mushy. Stir constantly to avoid burning. Add 1 cup of water and stir thoroughly. Stir in yogurt. Add garlic, cayenne pepper and salt. Stir thoroughly. Add remaining water. Bring to oil. Then turn heat to low and let simmer for 10 minutes.

***Nutritional note:*** *Turmeric has been reported to be helpful in treating diabetes, arthritis and liver disorders.*

## Cauliflower

4 cups cauliflower, chopped
1 cup yellow onion, chopped
2 T garlic powder
1 T turmeric
1 T black pepper
2 T olive oil
Dash of salt
½ cup water

Sauté onion in olive oil in sauce pan or skillet until caramelized. Add water and stir in cauliflower. Add garlic powder, turmeric, black pepper, and salt. Stir thoroughly. Add one more tablespoon of oil and or a little water, if needed. Bring to boil. Cover and simmer until cauliflower is as tender as desired.

*Nutritional note: Onions are known to be beneficial to eyes, hair, fingernails and toenails. They are also good for the sinus.*

## Veggie Medley Bake

2 cups potatoes, cubed
2 cups cauliflower, chopped
2 cups winter squash, chopped
1 cup celery, diced
1 cup onion, wedged
1 cup bread crumbs
1 cup vegetable broth
1 egg
1 cup plain yogurt
1 t turmeric
1 t sea salt
1 t pepper

Preheat oven at 375 degrees.

Spray roasting pan with non-sticking spray. Mix all ingredients into a bowl and stir thoroughly. Pour ingredients into large baking dish. Bake for 30 minutes or until potatoes are tender.

*Nutritional note: Salt is something we should be careful of because of the sodium content. But we also need enough sodium in optimal health. Adding a little salt to a well seasoned dish helps to magnify their flavors.*

## Rosemary Potatoes

4 cups potatoes, cubed
3 T rosemary, minced
2 T onion powder
2 T black pepper
2 T walnut oil
Pinch of sea salt

Pre-heat oven at 400 degrees.
Spray the bottom of a 9" X 13" baking pan with Pam. Mix all ingredients in large bowl. Make sure seasoning and oil are on all potatoes. Pour into pan. Add more seasoning to taste, if desired. Cook for 30 minutes or until potatoes are tender.

*Nutritional note: Rosemary has anti-inflammatory qualities. It is known to improve circulation and blood flow which helps the immune system and concentration.*

## Cabbage Soup

1 medium cabbage, chopped
2 cups tomatoes, diced
1 medium onion, diced
2 cups carrots, diced
½ cup cilantro, minced
3 T garlic powder

½ t sea salt
½ cayenne pepper
2 T olive oil
Water

Sauté onion in olive oil in large pot until tender and lightly caramelized. Add tomatoes and cook until soft. Add cup of water. Then add carrots. Add more water, if needed, to cover all carrots. Cook for about 5 minutes. Stir in cabbage. Add cilantro, garlic powder, sea salt and cayenne pepper. Stir well. Add more water, as needed and as desired. Turn heat to low and let simmer until cabbage has reached your desired tenderness.

Nutritional note: The cabbage is an eye strengthener. It helps to alleviate the mucous membranc of the intestine and stomach.

## Creamy Carrot Soup

4 cups of chopped carrots
1 T of onion, minced
1 T of parsley, minced
2 cups of water
1 t of garlic powder
½ t of cumin
½ t of sage
½ t of cayenne pepper
Pinch of sea salt
1 t walnut oil

Boil carrots and onion for 15 minutes. Add garlic powder, cumin, sage, cayenne pepper. Turn down heat to low and let simmer for 30 minutes or until carrots are soft. Test the softness by sticking them with a fork. When the fork penetrates through with no resistance, the carrots are ready. Pour all ingredients into blender along with parsley. Purée for 3 minutes or until creamy. Pour ingredients back unto pot. Add more water to thin the soup, if desired. Warm the soup on low temperature to heat for serving. Add walnut oil and salt. Stir well and serve.

This may be served as a side dish or with a salad. You may also add a sautéed meat of your choice and add to the soup.

*Nutritional note: Sage has anti-inflammatory and antioxidant properties. It is known to be a memory enhancer.*

## *Creamy Black Bean Soup*

4 cups black beans, cooked
1 cup tomatoes, diced
½ cup red onion, minced
2 T garlic powder
½ cup cilantro, minced
½ t cayenne pepper
Pinch of sea salt
1 cup of water

Put all ingredients in blender. Purée for 5 minutes. You may heat the soup for a few minutes in or order to serve it warm. You may add precooked beef, chicken or pork.

*Nutritional note: Cayenne pepper is a good source of Vitamin A. It has anti-inflammatory properties and is an immune booster.*

# Sandwiches, Pitas and Wraps

All of the sandwiches and pitas in this section are vegetarian. You may add whatever meat you desire to these sandwiches to suit your taste.

## Mushroom and Avocado Sandwich

2 slices of whole wheat bread
1 slice of cheddar cheese
2 T tomato sauce spread
1 T sautéed yellow onions, chopped
1 T sautéed (or jarred) mushrooms
1 T of avocado
2 slices of tomato
2 T lettuce, thinly sliced
1 T olive oil
1 T Worcestershire sauce

Sauté onion in olive oil until tender. Add Worcestershire sauce and mushrooms. Continue to sauté until onions are caramelized and mushrooms are tender. Remove pan from heat. Lightly toast bread. Spread tomato sauce spread onto bread. Layer sandwich with cheese, tomatoes, onions, mushrooms, avocado and lettuce.

## Tomato sauce spread

1 8 oz. can of tomato sauce
1 t basil flakes

1 t oregano flakes
Pinch of cayenne pepper
Pinch of sea salt

Mix all ingredients together. Stir thoroughly. Spread on bread. Put the remainder aside to use on your next sandwich.

**Nutritional note:** *We should always eat whole grain breads. Wheat is a great source of protein, iron and fiber.*

# Cucumber Sandwich

2 slices of whole wheat bread
6 slices cucumber
2 T red onion, thinly sliced
2 slices of tomato
2 T lettuce, thinly shredded
1 T cream cheese

Toast bread. Spread cream cheese onto each slice of bread. Layer sandwich with tomato, cucumber, onion and lettuce.

**Nutritional note:** *Cucumbers are so refreshing. They are known to improve the complexion of the skin and overall health of the skin.*

# Eggplant Sandwich

2 slices of whole wheat bread
1 slice of eggplant
1 slice Monterey jack cheese
2 slices tomato
1 T red onion, minced
1 T tomato sauce spread
2 T lettuce, thinly sliced
¼ t garlic powder
¼ t onion powder

¼ t black pepper
¼ t cayenne pepper
1 T olive oil

Preheat oven at 375 degrees.
Cut eggplant into ¼ inch slices. Season eggplant with garlic powder, onion powder, black pepper, cayenne pepper and olive oil. Bake for 15 minutes or until tender and done. Toast bread in toaster. Spread tomato sauce spread onto each slice of bread. (See directions with Mushroom and Avocado Sandwich.) Layer sandwich with cheese, eggplant, tomato, onion and lettuce.

***Nutritional note:*** *The eggplant is high in antioxidants. Studies have shown that it is helpful in lowering high blood pressure and bad cholesterol.*

## *Potato Sandwich*

2 slices whole wheat bread
4 slices of potato (adjust according to size of the potato)
1 T sun-dried tomatoes
1 slice cheddar cheese
2 T avocado, sliced
1 T green onion, diced
2 T lettuce, thinly sliced
1 T plain yogurt
¼ t garlic powder
¼ t onion powder
¼ t black pepper
¼ t cayenne pepper
1 T olive oil

Preheat oven 400 degrees.
Cut potato into ¼ inch slices. Season potatoes with garlic powder, onion powder, black pepper, cayenne pepper and olive oil. Bake potato slices for 15 minutes or until tender and done. Toast bread in toaster. Spread

yogurt on one slice of bread. Layer sandwich with cheese, potatoes, sundried tomatoes, avocado, onion and lettuce.

*Nutritional note: Onion helps to prevent blood clotting and lower bad cholesterol.*

## Tofu Sandwich

2 slices whole wheat bread
1 ¼ inch firm tofu slice
2 T lettuce, thinly sliced
1 T Dijon mustard
2 T yellow onion, diced
½ t jalapeno peppers, minced
2 slices tomato
1 T olive oil

Sauté onions in oil until tender. Add jalapeno peppers and sauté for 1 minute. Remove ingredients from skillet and set aside. Sauté tofu in same oil or add more, if needed. Cook for 1 minute on each side and remove from skillet. Toast bread in toaster or in skillet with remainder of the oil. Spread mustard on bread. Layer sandwich with tofu, tomatoes, onions, peppers and lettuce. Season with a little salt and pepper, if desired, and enjoy!

*Nutritional note: Tofu is an excellent source of protein and iron. Studies have found it to lower the LDL (bad) cholesterol and raise the HDL (good) cholesterol.*

## Artichoke and Mushroom Pita

2 artichoke hearts
4 olives, sliced
1 T sun-dried tomatoes, chopped
1 T red onion, thinly sliced
1 T red pepper, minced

1 T mushrooms, sliced
1 T avocado, sliced
1 slice Monterey jack
1 whole wheat pita

Put all ingredients in a bowl. Stir thoroughly. Carefully put into pita using your hands or a spoon. Sometimes the pita bread can be fragile.

*Nutritional note: Eating avocados can help to regulate blood pressure and lower the LDL (bad) cholesterol.*

## Avocado and Mushroom Pita

½ cup avocado, diced
2 T mushroom slices (jarred)
2 T tomato, largely diced
½ cup shredded lettuce
1 T red onion, thinly sliced
1 t olive oil
1 t basil
1 t garlic powder
1 whole wheat pita
Pinch of sea salt

Put all ingredients in a bowl. Stir thoroughly. Carefully put into pita using your hands or a spoon. Sometimes the pita bread can be fragile.

*Nutritional note: Mushrooms are a great source of selenium, Vitamin B2 and Vitamin B5.*

## Kale and Cucumber Pita

½ cup kale, chopped
½ cup lettuce, chopped
2 T cup cucumber, diced
2 T tomato, diced

2 T pecans, chopped
1 T cilantro, diced
1 T scallions, diced
1 T flaxseed oil
1 t garlic powder
1 whole wheat pita

Put all ingredients in a bowl. Stir thoroughly. Carefully put into pita using your hands or a spoon. Sometimes the pita bread can be fragile.

*Nutritional note: Pecans are high in antioxidants that help to combat LDL cholesterol and general weakness. They are a great source of potassium and protein.*

## Spinach and Sun-dried Tomato Pita

½ cup raw spinach, chopped
2 T Romaine lettuce, chopped
1 T artichoke hearts, chopped
1 T avocado, diced
1 T kalamata olives, chopped
1 T sun-dried tomatoes
1 T red onion, thinly sliced
1 t olive oil
1 t garlic powder
1 whole wheat pita

Put all ingredients in a bowl. Stir thoroughly. Carefully put into pita using your hands or a spoon. Sometimes the pita bread can be fragile.

*Nutritional note: Romaine lettuce is a great source of Vitamin K and fiber.*

## Kale and Artichoke Pita

½ cup kale, chopped

2 T lettuce, chopped
1 T artichoke hearts, diced
1 T red bell pepper, minced
2 T walnuts, chopped
1 T parsley, diced
1 T red onion, diced
1 t garlic powder
1 t olive oil
1 whole wheat pita

Put all ingredients in a bowl. Stir thoroughly. Carefully put into pita using your hands or a spoon. Sometimes the pita bread can be fragile.

*Nutritional note:* *Walnuts are a delicious source of Omega-3 fatty acids, protein and potassium. Studies have proven them to be very beneficial to the heart. One of those benefits is lowering the LDL (bad) cholesterol.*

## Tomato and Corn Pita

2 T avocado, diced
2 T tomato, diced
1 T corn
1 T peas
1 T scallions, diced
1 T parsley, minced
1 t olive oil
½ t cayenne pepper
1 whole wheat pita

Put all ingredients in a bowl. Stir thoroughly. Carefully put into pita using your hands or a spoon. Sometimes the pita bread can be fragile.

*Nutritional note:* *Corn is a good source of Vitamin B1, Vitamin B5 and fiber.*

## *Broccoli Pita*

½ cup broccoli, chopped
2 T tomatoes, diced
1 T red onion, thinly sliced
1 T pecans, chopped
1 T honey mustard
1 whole wheat pita

Put all ingredients in a bowl. Stir thoroughly. Carefully put into pita using your hands or a spoon. Sometimes the pita bread can be fragile.

*Nutritional note: Broccoli is an excellent source of calcium and fiber. It is a body detoxifier.*

## *Chicken and Pomegranate Wrap*

1 lb chicken breast, cooked and chopped
1 cup pomegranate seeds
½ cup pecans, chopped
½ cup green onions, diced
2 T cilantro, minced
2 T vinaigrette dressing
Pinch of salt
Pinch of pepper
4 kale leaves

Preheat oven at 375 degrees.
Season chicken with salt and pepper. Place in baking dish. Bake for 20 minutes or until done. Cut chicken unto small pieces. Mix all ingredients in a bowl. Stir thoroughly. Using a spoon carefully put ingredients into center fold of the kale leaves. And enjoy!

*Nutritional note: The juice from pomegranate seeds is packed with all kinds of powerful nutrients. It is said to help lower LDL (bad) cholesterol. It is recommended for overall heart health. Pomegranate juice has proven to prevent prostate cancer and slow down its growth. It reduces the risk of breast cancer.*

## Shrimp and Pineapple Wrap

1 lb shrimp, cooked
1 cup pineapple, finely chopped
2 T cilantro, minced
1 t garlic powder
1 T red pepper, minced
½ t ginger powder
Dash of salt
4 kale leaves

You may purchase the shrimp already cooked. Or you may quickly cook them in a little garlic powder and oil. Mix all ingredients in a bowl. Stir thoroughly. Using a spoon carefully put ingredients into center fold of the kale leaves. And enjoy!

**Nutritional note:** *Shrimp is an excellent source of selenium, Vitamin D, iron, protein and Vitamin B12.*

## Beef and Tomato Wrap

1 lb beef, cooked and chopped
1 cup tomatoes, chopped
2 T yellow onion, minced
2 T cilantro, minced
1 t garlic powder
4 large kale leaves
1 t garlic powder
½ t chili powder
Pinch of salt
Pinch of pepper

Preheat oven at 375 degrees.

Season meat with garlic powder, chili powder, salt and pepper. Bake meat for 20 minutes or until done. Cut into small pieces. Mix all ingredients in a bowl. Stir thoroughly. Using a spoon carefully put ingredients into center fold of the kale leaves. And enjoy!

**Nutritional note:** *Beef is one of the best sources of iron and protein. It is also recognized for it is supply of selenium and Vitamin B12.*

## Tuna Wrap

2 cups albacore tuna
2 T yellow onion, minced
2 T raisins
2 T apples, chopped
1 T plain yogurt
1 t pepper
Pinch of salt
4 large kale leaves

Mix all ingredients in a bowl. Stir thoroughly. Using a spoon carefully put ingredients into center fold of the kale leaves. And enjoy!

**Nutritional note:** *Tuna is an excellent source of selenium, protein, Vitamin B1, Vitamin B3 and Vitamin B6.*

## Veggie Wrap

1 cup avocado, chopped
1 cup tomatoes, chopped
1 cup mushrooms, cooked
2 T yellow onion, minced
1 T jalapeno, minced finely
Pinch of salt

Mix all ingredients in a bowl. Stir thoroughly. Using a spoon carefully put ingredients into center fold of the kale leaves. And enjoy!

**Nutritional note:** *Researchers have found that avocadoes contain the antioxidant, glutathione, which are beneficial to prevent aging, cancer and heart disease.*

## Potato and Chicken Wrap

2 cups chicken, cooked and chopped
1 cup potatoes, diced and cooked
1 cup tomatoes, diced
2 T parsley, minced
1 T green onion, minced
4 large kale leaves
1 T Cajun seasoning

Preheat oven at 375 degrees.
Dice potatoes into small pieces. Season chicken and potatoes with Cajun seasoning. Bake for 20 minutes or until done. Cut chicken into small pieces. Mix all ingredients in a bowl. Stir thoroughly. Using a spoon carefully put ingredients into center fold of the kale leaves. And enjoy!

**Nutritional note:** *Parsley is rich in antioxidants. Studies have proven it to be helpful in cases of colon cancer, heart disease and diabetes.*

# Smoothies and Juices

Juices and smoothies are so delightful. You should never throw away fresh vegetables and fruits. If you have a juicer or blender, throw them in there and make a healthy treat! I always use grapes, apples or banana to sweeten any juice or smoothie.

## Smoothies

### Banana Peach Smoothie

1 banana, peeled
1 peach, chopped (and peeled, if preferred)
1 mango, chopped (and peeled, if preferred)
2 t lemon juice
½ cup vanilla frozen yogurt (optional)

Put all ingredients in blender. Blend on the purée or liquefy speed until all ingredients are smooth in texture.

*Nutritional note: The skin of the mango and the peach are tasty and full of nutrients. This smoothie is good for high blood pressure and kidney health.*

### Pineapple Papaya Smoothie

2 cups pineapple, chopped
1 cup papaya, chopped

1 orange, chopped
2 ice cubes
½ cup of vanilla frozen yogurt

Pineapple: Cut the top and bottom off the pineapple first. Cut it in half. Shave the skin off of the pineapple. Cut around the core and discord it.

Papaya: Peel the skin with a knife. Remove the seeds from the papaya. You may put them aside. Allow them to dry and use them on salads.

Put all ingredients in a blender. Blend on the purée or liquefy speed until all ingredients are smooth in texture.

*Nutritional note: This smoothie is good for your colon and high blood pressure.*

## Avocado Smoothie

1 avocado, medium
1 banana
1 cup pineapple, chopped
1 t lime juice
½ cup vanilla frozen yogurt

Put all ingredients in a blender. Blend on the purée or liquefy speed until all ingredients are smooth in texture.

*Nutritional note: This smoothie is also good for the colon and high blood pressure.*

## Grape and Blueberry Smoothie

2 cups red grapes
1 cup blueberries
1 cup frozen vanilla yogurt or 2 cubes of ice

Wash grapes and blueberries thoroughly. Remove stems from grapes. Put all ingredients in a blender. Blend on the purée or liquefy speed until all ingredients are smooth in texture.

*Nutritional note: This smoothie is a blood and body cleanser.*

## Grape Apple Smoothie

2 cups green grapes
2 cups Fuji apples, cored and chopped
1 cup frozen vanilla yogurt and or 2 cubes of ice

Wash grapes and apples thoroughly. Remove stems from grapes. Remove core and chop apples. Put all ingredients in a blender. Blend on the purée or liquefy speed until all ingredients are smooth in texture.

*Nutritional note: This smoothie is good for kidney health and promotes healthy skin.*

## Raspberry Strawberry Smoothie

1 cup strawberries
1 cup raspberries
1 cup red grapes
2 ice cubes
1 cup frozen vanilla yogurt

Thoroughly wash strawberries, raspberries and red grapes. Remove leaves and stem from strawberries. Remove stems from grapes. Put all ingredients in a blender. Blend on the purée or liquefy speed until all ingredients are smooth in texture.

*Nutritional note: This smoothie is good for high blood pressure and healthy skin.*

## Blackberry Blueberry Smoothie

½ cup blueberries
½ cup blackberries
1 cup red grapes
2 ice cubes

Wash blueberries, blackberries and grapes thoroughly. Remove stems from grapes. Put all ingredients in a blender. Blend on the purée or liquefy speed until all ingredients are smooth in texture.

Other options:
1 cup vanilla yogurt—You may add this to the mixture above or in place of the grapes.
1 banana—You may add this along with the yogurt or just in place of the grapes.
½ cup grape juice—You may add this to any of the combinations in place of the grapes
½ plain yogurt—You may use this instead of the vanilla yogurt. This yogurt goes well with the banana. protein powder—This goes well with the banana combination.

*Nutritional note: This smoothie is a blood and body cleanser.*

## Berry Medley

½ cup strawberries
½ cup raspberries
½ cup blackberries
½ cup blueberries
½ cup organic apple cider
½ cup frozen vanilla yogurt
2 cubes of ice

Wash strawberries, raspberries, blackberries and blueberries thoroughly. Cut off stems and leaves from strawberries. Put all ingredients in a blender. Blend on the purée or liquefy speed until all ingredients are smooth in texture.

*Nutritional note: This smoothie is good for high blood pressure, blood cleansing and kidney health.*

## Green Smoothie

2 cups kale (or any leafy green vegetable)
½ avocado
1 banana, peeled
¼ cup organic apple cider

Wash kale thoroughly. Remove peel and seed from avocado. Put all ingredients in a blender. Blend on the purée or liquefy speed until all ingredients are smooth in texture.

Other options to replace kale: spinach, collards greens, turnip greens, mustard greens, dandelion greens or beet greens.

*Nutritional note: Bananas are a good source of energy. Eating a banana in the morning should give you a good boast of energy in the morning as well as lots of potassium.*

## Banana Nut Smoothie

1 banana
½ cup walnuts
1 cup vanilla yogurt
2 ice cubes

Put all ingredients in a blender. Blend on the purée or liquefy speed until all ingredients are smooth in texture.

*Nutritional note: This smoothie is good for high blood pressure and general energy.*

# Juices

## Carrot Orange Juice

4 large carrots
1 orange
½ lemon
1 T ginger juice

Thoroughly wash the carrots or peel them. Remove the stem. Peel orange and break into pieces. Peel lemon. Wash ginger root and remove all dark brown spots. I recommend juicing at least 1 pound of ginger root at a time, so that you will have more on hand when needed to add to your juices. Ginger juice is great in teas also. Cut all ingredients to fit into your juicer. Juice all of the ingredients and enjoy!

*Nutritional note:* *This juice is good for hair, nails skin, high blood pressure, bladder, kidneys, obesity and blood cleansing.*

## Beet Carrot Juice

1 medium beets, chopped
2 large carrots
1 cup pineapple, pieces
1 cup strawberries
½ lemon
1 T ginger juice

Wash beets and carrots thoroughly. Remove any excess tiny roots. Chop into small pieces. Remove leafy stem from the top of strawberries. Wash thoroughly. Wash and remove all dark brown spots from ginger root. Cut away skin and core from pineapple. Cut all ingredients to fit into your juicer. Juice and enjoy!

*Greta Andrews*

*Nutritional note: This juice is good for anemia, menstrual problems, hair, nails skin, high blood pressure, bladder, kidneys, obesity and blood cleansing.*

## Cabbage Juice

2 cups cabbage, chopped
1 green apple, cored and chopped
1 cup green grapes
½ lime
1 T ginger juice

Thoroughly wash cabbage. Cut one fourth of cabbage. Cut into squares that will fit your juicer. Holding cabbage leaves together, juice the cabbage and set aside. Juice apple, grapes, lime and ginger root. Mix all ingredients together and enjoy! You may use ginger ale in place of the ginger juice. Add enough to modify taste as desired.

*Nutritional note: Cabbage juice has been proven to heal stomach ulcers. If you have ulcers, prepare this recipe for seven days and you should experience an improvement in your condition. If you choose to use the cabbage juice to aid in your healing, make sure that your physician is aware and involved.*

## Cucumber Juice

1 large cucumber
2 cups raw spinach leaves
1 large carrot
2 cups lettuce
1 medium apple
1 cup green grapes
½ lime

Thoroughly wash all ingredients. Cut all ingredients to fit your juicer. Peel the rind off lime with your hand or using a knife. Juice all ingredients, mix together and enjoy.

*Nutritional note: This juice contains cucumber, spinach, carrot and lettuce juices that have proven to be helpful in making the hair to grow.*

## Cantaloupe and Carrot Juice

1 cup cantaloupe
2 large carrots
1 peach
1 cup pineapple
1 orange

Thoroughly wash the cantaloupe, carrots and peach. Remove seed from peach. Cut the skin and core from the pineapple. Peel orange with hands or a knife. Using a knife makes it better for juicing. Cut all ingredients into pieces that will fit your juicer. You may juice the cantaloupe with the rind still on. It still tastes great! Juice and enjoy!

*Nutritional note: This recipe is designed to help with high blood pressure.*

## Cucumber and Celery Juice

1 cucumber
2 celery stalks
1 pear
1 cup pineapple

Thoroughly wash the cucumber, celery stalks, and pear. Remove the skin and the core from the pineapple. Remove core and stem from the pear. Cut all ingredients to fit your juicer. Juice and enjoy!

***Nutritional note:*** *This juice is also designed to help with high blood pressure.*

## Papaya and Pineapple Juice

2 carrots
1 cup cantaloupe
1 cup papaya
1 cup pineapple
1 orange
½ lemon

Thoroughly wash carrots and cantaloupe. Cut the papaya in half and remove the seeds. You may set the seeds aside to add to a salad later. Remove seeds from cantaloupe. You may juice the cantaloupe with the rind. Cut the skin and core from the pineapple. Peel the orange and lemon with hands or knife. Cut all ingredients into pieces that will fit your juicer and juice.

***Nutritional note:*** *This juice is designed to help with flushing fat from the body.*

## Beet and Apple Juice

2 medium beets
1 apple
1 cup cantaloupe
1 cup mango
1 cup strawberries

Thoroughly wash beets, apples, cantaloupe and strawberries. Cut stem from beets and all access roots. Remove core from apple. Remove leafy stems from strawberries. Remove skin and core from mango. Remove seeds from cantaloupe. You may juice cantaloupe with rind. Cut all ingredients to fit your juicer and juice. This is a beautiful and tasty juice! Don't let the beets deter you. They are very sweet!

*Nutritional note: This juice is designed to help promote kidney health.*

## Beet and Strawberry Juice

2 medium beets
2 large carrots
1 peach
1 cup strawberries
1 tangerine

Wash beets, carrots, peach and strawberries thoroughly. Remove any access stem or roots from beets or carrots. Remove seed from peach. Cut away all leafy stems from strawberries. Peel tangerines. Cut all ingredients to fit your juicer. Juice and enjoy!

*Nutritional note: This juice is designed to promote liver health.*

## Apple and Peach Juice

1 apple
1 cup cantaloupe
1 large carrot
1 peach
1 pear
1 tangerine
½ lemon
2 T ginger juice

Thoroughly wash apple, cantaloupe, carrot, peach, pear and ginger root. Remove core from apple and pear. Remove seeds from cantaloupe. Remove any access stem or roots from carrot. Remove seed from peach. Peel tangerine with hands. Peel lemon with hands or knife, preferably with a knife. Wash and remove all dark brown spots from ginger root. Cut all ingredients to fit your juicer and juice.

*Nutritional note:* This juice is designed to nourish healthy skin.

## Apple and Carrot Juice

2 apples
2 carrots
1 medium beet
½ lemon
1 T ginger juice

Thoroughly wash apples, carrots, beets and ginger root. Remove stem and core from apples. Remove any access from stems or roots or carrots and beets. Peel lemon with hands or knife, preferably a knife. Wash and remove all dark brown spots from ginger root. Cut all ingredients to fit your juicer and juice them.

*Nutritional note:* This juice is designed to enhance healthy hair.

# Sweet Treats

Finding a healthy sweet treat can be challenging. I have put together a few recipes that I have found to be tasteful and at the same time healthy. None of these treats call for white sugar, enriched flour or butter. Because all of these muffins are made without sugar, they will not be as sweet as you are used to. I usually make a muffin glaze to cover the top of the muffin. I will give you the recipe for the glaze first. You may add other flavors or fruit to the glaze to go with that particular muffin.

## *Muffin Glaze*

3 T walnut oil
2 T honey
1 T cinnamon

Mix the ingredients together until consistent. Baste onto the muffins as desired.

## *Loaded Muffins*

3 cups whole wheat flour
2 cups muesli
2 cups sweet purée mix (½ cup dates, ½ cup raisins, ½ cup prunes, ½ cup water)
1 ½ cups yogurt
2 eggs
4 T cinnamon
1 ¼ t baking soda
2 cup walnuts, chopped

½ cup apple cider
1 cup apple sauce
2 T honey
¼ t sea salt

Preheat oven at 400 degrees.
Prepare muffin pan. Use non-stick muffin pan or Pam on regular muffin pan.
Chop walnuts and set aside. Purée dates, raisins, prunes and water and set aside.
Mix flour, cinnamon, baking soda and salt and mix thoroughly. Add purée and yogurt and stir. Add muesli and stir thoroughly. Add apple cider, apple juice and honey and stir. Add walnuts and stir. Pour batter into muffin pan and bake for 20 minutes.

**Nutritional note:** *Prunes are a great source of Vitamin A and potassium. They help to improve blood circulation and help to relieve constipation.*

## Oatmeal Raisin Muffins

3 cups whole wheat flour
1 cup oatmeal, cooked
2 cups apple sauce
2 cups raisins
2 cups walnuts, chopped
2 cups yogurt
1 t baking powder
2 eggs
¼ cup cinnamon
¼ cup walnut oil
¼ cup honey
¼ t sea salt

Preheat oven at 400 degrees.
Prepare muffin pan. Use non-stick muffin pan or Pam on regular muffin pan.

Cook oatmeal and set to the side. In a large mixing bowl combine flour, baking powder, salt and cinnamon. Stir in milk using hands or mixer on medium speed. Fold in oatmeal incrementally. Add apple sauce and stir. Add eggs and stir. Add walnut oil and honey and stir. Mix ingredients until smooth and consistent. Add raisins and walnuts. Mix thoroughly. Pour into muffin pan and bake for 30 minutes.

*Nutritional note: Oatmeal is high in antioxidants. It is beneficial for heart health. It is a great source of fiber.*

## Strawberry Pecan Muffins

3 cups whole wheat flour
2 cups strawberries, puréed
1 cup apple sauce
2 cup organic unfiltered apple cider or juice
1 cup plain yogurt
2 eggs
2 cups pecans, chopped
1 ¼ t baking powder
3 T cinnamon
3 T honey
¼ t sea salt

Preheat oven at 400 degrees.
Prepare muffin pan. Use non-stick muffin pan or Pam on regular muffin pan.
Purée strawberries and chop pecans and put to the side. Mix flour, baking powder, cinnamon and salt in a large mixing bowl. Pour in apple cider and mix with large spoon or mixer on medium speed. Pour in apple sauce and stir. Pour in yogurt and eggs and stir. Add honey, strawberries and pecans. Stir thoroughly. Pour into muffin pan and bake for 30 minutes.

*Nutritional note: Strawberries are blood and skin cleansers. They are helpful in cases of high blood pressure, gout, rheumatism and skin cancer.*

## Lemon Muffins

3 cups whole wheat flour
1 cup lemon juice
½ cup lemon zest
1 cup apple sauce
½ cup apple juice
1 ½ cup yogurt
2 eggs
1 ½ t baking soda
¼ cup honey
3 T cinnamon
1 cup almonds, chopped
¼ t sea salt

Preheat oven at 400 degrees.
Prepare muffin pan. Use non-stick muffin pan or Pam on regular muffin pan.
Use citrus juicer to extract juice from at least 3 lemons to get 1 cup of lemon juice and set aside. Use grater on lemons to get zest and set aside. Chop almonds and set aside.
Mix flour, baking soda and salt in a large mixing bowl. Pour in lemon juice and apple juice and mix using large spoon or mixer on medium speed. Pour in apple sauce and stir. Add eggs and stir. Add yogurt, cinnamon and honey and stir. Mix until smooth and consistent. Add zest and almonds and stir. Pour batter into muffin pan and bake for 30 minutes.

**Nutritional note:** *Strawberries are blood and skin cleansers. They are helpful in cases of high blood pressure, gout, rheumatism and skin cancer.*

## Pineapple Coconut Muffins

3 cups whole wheat flour
1 cup crushed pineapple
1 cup coconut flakes

1 cup pineapple juice
1 cup coconut milk
1 cup plain yogurt
2 T coconut flavor
2 T honey
1 cup macadamia nuts, chopped
2 eggs
½ t baking soda
¼ t sea salt

Preheat oven at 400 degrees.
Prepare muffin pan. Use non-stick muffin pan or Pam on regular muffin pan.
Chop macadamia nuts and set aside.
Mix flour, baking soda and salt in a large mixing bowl. Pour in pineapple juice and milk and stir. Add pineapple, coconut flakes, yogurt mix thoroughly. Add in eggs and stir. Stir in coconut flavor and honey and stir. Pour in macadamia nuts. Stir thoroughly. Pour batter into muffin pan and bake for 30 minutes.

*Nutritional note: The coconut is recommended in cases of inflammation of the large intestines, constipation and thyroid gland problems. Macadamia nuts are excellent for anemia and general weakness.*

## Blueberry Muffins

3 cups whole wheat flour
2 cups blueberries
1 cup dates puréed
1 ½ cup yogurt
2 eggs
1 t baking soda
2 T cinnamon
3 T honey
2 cups pecans, chopped
¼ t salt

Preheat oven at 400 degrees.

Prepare muffin pan. Use non-stick muffin pan or Pam on regular muffin pan.

Purée dates and set aside. Chop pecans and set aside.

Mix flour, baking soda, cinnamon and salt in a large mixing bowl. Pour in date purée, honey and yogurt and mix thoroughly. Add eggs and stir. Stir in blueberries and pecans. Pour batter into muffin pan and bake for 30 minutes.

*Nutritional note: Dates is one of the highest sources of potassium, which makes it valuable to regulating blood pressure.*

## Blackberry Muffins

2 cups whole wheat flour
2 cups blackberries
1 cup dates and prunes puréed
1 cup yogurt
2 eggs
1 ¼ t baking soda
1 T cinnamon
2 T honey
2 cups walnuts, chopped
¼ t sea salt

Preheat oven at 400 degrees.

Prepare muffin pan. Use non-stick muffin pan or Pam on regular muffin pan.

Purée dates and prunes and set aside. Chop nuts and set aside.

Mix flour, baking soda, cinnamon and salt in large mixing bowl. Pour in purée, honey and yogurt and mix thoroughly. Add eggs and stir. Stir in blackberries and walnuts. Mix thoroughly. Pour batter into muffin pan and bake for 30 minutes.

*Nutritional note: Prunes are a great source of Vitamin A and potassium. They are excellent for improving the blood circulation and vitality. They are beneficial to individuals suffering from anemia, constipation and hemorrhoids.*

## Chocolate Muffins

2 cups whole wheat flour
½ cup cocoa
1 cup yogurt
1 cup dates puréed
2 eggs
1 t baking soda
2 cups walnuts chopped
1 T pure vanilla flavor
¼ t sea salt

Preheat oven at 400 degrees.
Prepare muffin pan. Use non-stick muffin pan or Pam on regular muffin pan.
Mix flour, baking soda and salt in a large mixing bowl. Add vanilla flavor, yogurt and purée and mix thoroughly. Stir in eggs. Fold in cocoa incrementally. Add walnuts and stir thoroughly. Pour into muffin pan and bake for 30 minutes.

***Nutritional note:*** *Studies have proven that cocoa is beneficial to heart health. They increase blood flow and prevent clogging of the arteries.*

## Banana Nut Muffins

3 cups whole wheat flour
2 cups bananas, mashed
1 cup yogurt
½ cup applesauce
2 eggs
2 T cinnamon
1 t baking soda
2 cups walnuts, chopped

¼ t sea salt

Preheat oven at 400 degrees.
Prepare muffin pan. Use non-stick muffin pan or Pam on regular muffin pan.
Mash bananas until soft and set aside. Chop walnuts and set aside.
Mix flour, cinnamon, baking soda and salt in a large mixing bowl. Add yogurt and applesauce and mix thoroughly. Add eggs and stir thoroughly. Add bananas and walnuts. Stir thoroughly. Pour into muffin pan or loaf. Bake for 30 minutes.

*Nutritional note:* Applesauce is a more health substitute for white sugar and butter. It is a good source of fiber.

# More Treats

### Pomegranate Pecan Snack

½ cup pecans, chopped
½ cup pomegranate seeds

Always use equal parts of pecans and pomegranate seeds to make whatever amount desired. Mix together and enjoy.

*Nutritional note:* Pomegranate seeds are a good source of fiber. The juice contributes to good heart health. It fights prostate and breast cancer.

### Pomegranate Carrot Snack

½ cup pecans, chopped
½ cup pomegranate seeds
1 cup carrots, raw and cubed
1 T ground cinnamon

1 t honey

Mix carrots, cinnamon and honey together. Mix pecans and pomegranates seeds and place on top of the carrot mix.

*Nutritional note: Carrots are one of the best sources of Vitamin A. Cinnamon is beneficial in treating Type 2 diabetes.*

## Sweet Potato Apple Snack

½ cup sweet potato, cubed
½ cup apple, cubed
½ cup pecans, chopped
1 T honey
1 T ground cinnamon

Mix all ingredients together until honey and cinnamon are evenly distributed in mixture. Enjoy this refreshing and delightful treat!

*Nutritional note: Sweet potatoes are an excellent source of Vitamin A and potassium. They are helpful in cases of inflammation of the colon and stomach ulcers. They contribute to heart health and help to improve blood circulation.*

## Very Berry Sorbet

½ cup blackberries, frozen
½ cup blueberries, frozen
½ cup raspberries, frozen
½ cup strawberries, frozen
1 cup Organic Apple Cider
1 T honey
1 t lemon juice

Put all ingredients in your blender. Blend ingredients on the puree speed. Use spoon to move ingredients around in blender. Add more honey to sweeten, if needed, since berries can be bitter.

***Nutritional note:*** *All of the berries above are considered to be blood cleansers. Apple cider helps to prevent kidney stones.*

# Breakfast Foods

Most of the recipes in this section include eggs. They are so beneficial to our health and should be consumed on a regular basis to get the protein, iron and other valuable nutrients that we need daily. You may add any choice of meat to your egg scramble.

## *Scrambled Turmeric Eggs*

2 eggs
½ t garlic powder
½ t turmeric
Pinch of black pepper
Pinch of sea salt
1 T canola oil

Heat oil in small skillet. Crack eggs into small mixing bowl. Add garlic powder, turmeric, black pepper and sea salt. Whip seasonings into eggs with a fork or whisk. Pour eggs into skillet and cook as desired.

*Nutritional note: Eggs are one of the best sources of protein and iron. We need 50 grams of protein per day. One average egg contains 17 grams. Consuming 2 eggs will give you 34 grams.*

## *Southwest Scramble*

3 eggs
1 T onions, diced
1 T red bell pepper, diced
1 T green bell pepper, diced

2 T tomatoes, diced
1 T canola oil
½ t garlic powder
½ t turmeric
½ t black pepper
Pinch of sea salt

Crack eggs into small mixing bowl. Add garlic powder, turmeric, black pepper and sea salt. Whip seasonings into eggs using fork or whisk. Put eggs to the side. Sauté onions in a skillet until tender. Add green and red bell peppers and sauté them for 1 minute. Add eggs and scramble them to desired texture.

*Nutritional note: Eggs contain biotin which aids preventing hair from turning gray. It is beneficial in helping to treat baldness.*

## Spinach and Mushroom Scramble

3 eggs
½ cup spinach
½ cup mushrooms, sliced
½ cup tomatoes, diced
1 T yellow onions, minced
½ t turmeric
½ t black pepper
Pinch of salt
1 T canola oil

Crack eggs into small mixing bowl. Add turmeric, black pepper and sea salt. Whip seasonings into eggs using fork or whisk. Put eggs to the side. Sauté onions in oil in skillet until slightly limp. Add mushrooms and cook until tender. Add tomatoes and sauté with mixture for a few seconds. Add spinach and cook until limp. Remove ingredients from skillet and place on plate. Add more oil, if needed, and cook eggs as desired. Put eggs on top of other ingredients and enjoy!

*Nutritional note: The biotin in eggs helps to treat eczema and dermatitis.*

## Artichoke and Spinach Scramble

3 eggs
½ cup artichoke hearts, chopped
½ cup spinach
1 T yellow onions, minced
2 T Monterey jack cheese, grated
½ t turmeric
½ t black pepper
Pinch of sea salt
1 T canola oil

Crack eggs into small mixing bowl. Add turmeric, black pepper and sea salt. Whip seasonings into eggs using fork or whisk. Put eggs to the side. Sauté onions in oil in a skillet until tender. Stir in artichoke hearts. Add spinach and cook for a few seconds until limp. Stir in cheese. Allow to lightly melt and remove with all ingredients from the skillet. Place in a bowl. Add more oil, if needed, and cook eggs. Place eggs on plate. Put other ingredients on top of eggs and enjoy.

***Nutritional note:*** *Egg yolks contain choline which helps prevent cholesterol buildup. It has proven to be beneficial in treating Alzheimer's disease. Choline aids the liver by ridding the body of poisons and drugs. It also enhances the memory.*

## Kale and Sun-Dried Tomato Scramble

3 eggs
½ cup kale, chopped
½ cup sun-dried tomatoes
2 T Monterey cheese, grated
1 T yellow onion, chopped
½ t turmeric
½ t garlic powder
Pinch of black pepper
Pinch of sea salt
1 T canola oil

Crack eggs into small mixing bowl. Add garlic powder, turmeric, black pepper and sea salt. Whip seasonings into eggs using fork or whisk. Put eggs to the side. Sauté onion in oil in skillet until tender. Add kale and sauté until tender. Stir in sun-dried tomatoes. Add cheese and allow it to lightly melt. Remove ingredients from skillet and put in plate. Add more oil to skillet, if needed, and cook eggs as desired. Put eggs on top of other ingredients and enjoy!

*Nutritional note: Eggs are a good source of Vitamin A which helps to strengthen weak eyesight and helps the immune system work properly.*

## Shrimp and Artichoke Scramble

3 eggs
1 cup raw shrimp
½ cup artichoke, chopped
½ cup sun-dried tomatoes, chopped
1 T green onion, diced
2 T Monterey cheese, grated
½ t turmeric
½ t black pepper
Pinch of sea salt
1 T cooking oil

Crack eggs into small mixing bowl. Add garlic powder, turmeric, black pepper and sea salt. Whip seasonings into eggs using fork or whisk. Put eggs to the side. Cook shrimp in oil in a skillet until done. Add eggs and cook to desired texture. Remove skillet from heat and add artichoke, sundried tomatoes and green onion. Add cheese and cover until cheese is lightly melted. Pour ingredients onto plate and enjoy!

*Nutritional note: Eggs contain Vitamin B2 which enhances the health of hair, skin and nails.*

# Cucumber and Tomato Scramble

3 eggs
1 T green onions, diced
1 T red bell pepper, diced
1 T green bell pepper, diced
2 T tomatoes, diced
2 T cucumber, diced
1 T parsley, minced
1 T canola oil
½ t turmeric
½ t black pepper
Pinch of sea salt

Mix green onions, red bell pepper, green bell pepper, tomatoes, parsley and cucumber in a bowl. Set aside. Crack eggs into small mixing bowl. Add turmeric, black pepper and sea salt. Whip seasonings into eggs using fork or whisk. Cook eggs in oil to desired texture. Put eggs in a plate and the vegetable mixture on top.

*Nutritional note: Eggs contain Vitamin B6 which helps to fight nervous and skin disorders. It has anti-aging properties.*

# Sunrise Breakfast Taco

3 eggs
1 T green onion, diced
2 T cheddar cheese, grated
½ t chili powder
½ t turmeric
½ t black pepper
Pinch of salt
1 T cooking oil
2 corn tortillas
2 T salsa
1 T lettuce, finely shredded

Heat oil in skillet. Crack eggs into small mixing bowl. Add chili powder, turmeric, black pepper and sea salt. Whip seasonings into eggs using fork or whisk. Cook eggs to desired texture. Remove eggs from skillet and put in bowl to the side. Heat tortillas in skillet just enough to get them warm. Place tortillas side by side on plate. Put equal parts of eggs on tortillas. Top with green onion, salsa and cheese.

*Nutritional note: Eggs are a good source of Vitamin B12 which helps to fight anemia. It promotes a healthy nervous system. Vitamin B12 enhances concentration, memory and balance.*

## Breakfast Kale Wrap

2 eggs
½ t turmeric
1 T onion, diced
1 t green bell pepper, diced
1 t red bell pepper, diced
Pinch of sea salt
1 T salsa
1 T plain yogurt
2 kale leaves

Crack eggs into small mixing bowl. Add turmeric and stir with a fork. Set eggs aside. Heat oil in skillet. Sauté onion, red bell pepper and green bell pepper until slightly limp. Stir in eggs and scramble as desired. Using a spoon carefully put ingredients into center fold of the kale leaves. Top ingredients with salsa and yogurt and enjoy!

*Nutritional note: Eggs contain Vitamin E which keeps us looking younger. It prevents blood clots and eliminates fatigue.*

## Breakfast Potatoes

3 cups potatoes, cubed
½ cup onion, diced

½ cup green bell pepper, diced
½ cup red bell pepper, diced
½ cup yogurt plain
1 T milk
1 T garlic powder
1 t black pepper
½ t sea salt
1 cup Colby cheese, shredded
1 T olive oil

Preheat oven at 400 degrees.
Mix all ingredients, except cheese, in a large bowl and stir thoroughly. Spray baking dish with non-stick spray. Pour ingredients into baking dish and cook for 30 minutes or until potatoes are done. Put cheese on top of potatoes while potatoes are still hot and cover for a couple of minutes until the cheese melts.

*Nutritional note: Potatoes are a great source of Vitamin C which promotes healing. It helps to prevent blood clots.*

## Granola Nut Mix Cereal

1 cup of granola cereal
7 cashews, raw
1 t sunflower seeds, raw
1 t ground cinnamon
½ cup milk (soy, almond or regular)

Mix all ingredients in a bowl and enjoy.

*Nutritional note: Sunflower seeds nourish the entire body. They promote healthy eyes, fingernails, teeth and skin.*

# Nutritional Guide

## Vitamins and Minerals

This section will help you to cater your diet to the vitamins that you need and are focused on for your health. I have listed good sources for you and the daily recommended intake. Be aware of toxicity levels so that you can accomplish your goals without side effects.

**Vitamin A**—Vitamin A helps to keep the outer layers of tissues and organs healthy. It is known as a wrinkle eliminator and helps to remove age spots. Vitamin A is reported to improve eyesight and counteracts night blindness. It promotes growth, strong bones, healthy skin, hair, teeth, and gums. It is said to aid in the treatment of emphysema and hyperthyroidism. Vitamin A resists respiratory infections and aids the immune system in functioning properly.
**Good sources:** Fish liver oil, liver, carrots, parsley, spinach, beet greens, mustard greens, kale, endive, dandelion greens, turnip greens, broccoli, lettuce, cabbage, watercress, apricots, peaches, peas, beans, papaya, sweet potatoes, dried prunes, asparagus, sweet corn, oranges, cantaloupes, pecans, chicken, cheeses and milk products.
**Recommended daily intake**: 4,000—5,000 IU daily
**Toxicity:** 50,000 IU daily for several months and 18,500 IU daily for infants

**Vitamin B1**—This Vitamin is also known as Thiamine. All of the Vitamin B's are synergistic and are more potent when taken together. Vitamin B1 helps the body to resist diseases and it aids in metabolizing carbohydrates so that they can be converted into energy. It is said to improve your mental attitude and aids the nervous system, muscles and heart in functioning normally.

**Good sources:** Whole grains, oatmeal, peanuts, organic meats, lean pork, bran, milk, black walnuts, Brazil nuts, hazel nuts.

**Recommended daily intake**: 1.5 mg. daily

**Toxicity:** Possibly 5—10 grams


**Vitamin B2**—Also known as Riboflavin and Vitamin G, this vitamin aids in reproduction and growth. It is reported to help promote healthy hair, skin and nails. Vitamin B2 contributes to eye health by alleviating eye fatigue. It also aids in metabolizing carbohydrates, proteins and fats.

**Good sources:** Milk, liver, yeast, cheese, fish, eggs, turnips, beets, dandelions, broccoli, carrots, coconuts, grapefruits, lemons, apples, watercress, blueberries, leafy green vegetables.

**Recommended daily intake**: 1.7 mg. daily

**Toxicity:** No known toxicity level


**Vitamin B6**—Vitamin B6, also known as pyridoxine, helps to prevent tooth decay. Because this vitamin has a soothing effect on the nerves, it can be used to control nervousness. Vitamin B6 helps to alleviate nausea and is used to aid in cases of morning sickness. Studies have shown that this vitamin is of great value for the pancreas to function properly. It is required for the proper production of red blood cells and antibodies.

**Good sources:** Liver, eggs, whole wheat, soy beans, cantaloupe, cabbage, oats, peanuts, walnuts, honey, corn oil, fish.

**Recommended daily intake**: 1.6—2.0 mg. daily

**Toxicity:** 2—10 grams can possibly result in neurological disorders. It is not recommended to consume any dosages over 500 mg.


**Vitamin B12**—Vitamin B12 which is also known as cobalamin, helps to prevent anemia by forming and regenerating red blood cells. This vitamin helps to increase energy and relieves irritability. Vitamin B12 is vital to the nervous system because it depends on this vitamin for nutrition. It helps to improve balance, concentration and memory.

**Good sources**—Beef, pork, liver, eggs, milk, cheese, kidney, oyster, salt-water fish.

**Recommended daily intake**: 2 mcg. daily
**Toxicity**—No known toxicity level

**Vitamin B13**—It has been reported that Vitamin B13 can aid in preventing liver ailments and aging prematurely. It is also said to help in treating multiple sclerosis.
**Good sources**—Whey, root vegetables, buttermilk and curdled milk (the liquid portion).
**Recommended daily intake**: None is established.
**Toxicity**—No known toxicity level due to lack of research

**Vitamin B15**—Vitamin B15 is not one of the more popular vitamins but it can be very helpful in one's diet. It has been reported that this vitamin can extend the life span of cells and can aid in recovering from fatigue speedily. It is said to help relieve the symptoms of asthma and angina. Vitamin B15 is beneficial in helping to lower bad cholesterol.
**Good sources**—Whole brown rice, whole grains, pumpkin seeds, sesame seeds.
**Recommended daily intake**: None established. Doses are usually 50—150 mg. daily.
**Toxicity**—No known toxicity level due to lack of research

**Vitamin C**—Vitamin C is the most commonly used vitamin. This vitamin plays an important role in the formation of collagen, which is vital for the repair and growth of body tissue cells. This vitamin aids in healing wounds, burns and bleeding gums. Vitamin C is best known for being beneficial in fighting the common cold, influenza, many types of viral and bacterial infections and boosting the immune system. It helps lower bad cholesterol and lowers blood clot incidents in veins. Vitamin C helps the body absorb iron and should be taken with calcium and magnesium to maximize its effectiveness. It has been reported that this vitamin protects against cancer producing agents.
**Good sources**—Guava, kale, parsley, collard greens, mustard greens, spinach, turnip greens, broccoli, cauliflower, Brussels sprouts, watercress, tomatoes, oranges, lemons, grapefruits, papaya, strawberries.
**Recommended daily intake**: The RDA is 60 mg. daily, but some supplements are as high as 5,000 mg.

**Toxicity**—Very high doses of 10 grams have been reported to cause side effects of diarrhea, skin rashes and excessive urination.

**Vitamin D**—Vitamin D is also called the "the sunshine vitamin" because you can an ample amount of the requirement of this vitamin with as little as ten to twenty minutes of sunshine per day. This vitamin regulates the proper absorption of calcium and phosphorus. It aids in the assimilation of Vitamin A. Vitamin D promotes the normal development of bones and teeth. A deficiency of this vitamin could result in severe tooth decay and a disease known as rickets. This vitamin is reported to aid in cases of conjunctivitis.
**Good sources**—Sunshine, fish oils, sardines, salmon, tuna, eggs, herring, Vitamin D-fortified dairy products.
**Recommended daily intake**: 200-400 IU daily
**Toxicity**—20,000 IU daily in adults and 1,800 IU daily in children

**Vitamin E**—Vitamin E is an antioxidant that helps to keep you looking young. It can alleviate fatigue and is able to convert excess fat into energy. This vitamin is necessary to regulate the proper levels of normal red blood cells. It has been reported that Vitamin E protects the body from infections and viruses. Vitamin E is said to play an important role in heart health by lowering blood pressure, lowering the risk of ischemic heart disease, and preventing and dissolving blood clots.
**Good sources**—Wheat germ, eggs, soybeans, vegetable oils, nuts, Brussels sprouts, leafy greens, spinach, whole wheat, whole grains, brown rice, barley, rye, beans, lentils, peas.
**Recommended daily intake**: The RDA is 10 IU daily. Supplements are usually up to 1,500 IU.
**Toxicity**—No known toxic level

**Vitamin F**—This vitamin prevents the buildup of cholesterol deposits in the arteries. It has been reported to combat heart disease. Vitamin F aids in promoting healthy skin and hair.
**Good sources**—Wheat germ oil, peanut oil, olive oil, soybean oil, safflower oil, peanuts, sunflower seeds, walnuts, pecans, almonds, avocados, fish oil.
**Recommended daily intake**: No RDA is established. Supplements are available 100—150 mg.

**Toxicity**—No known toxic level.

**Vitamin H**—Vitamin H, which is also known as biotin, is considered to be part of the Vitamin B-complex group. Two wonderful characteristics of this vitamin are that it can aid in helping to keep hair from turning gray and preventing baldness. It is said to help alleviate dermatitis and eczema.
**Good sources**—Egg yolks, beef liver, milk, yeast.
**Recommended daily**: None is established. Doses are usually 100—150 mg.
**Toxicity**—No known toxic level

**Vitamin K**—Vitamin K is mainly known for aiding the blood to clot in order to stop internal bleeding and hemorrhaging. It is a common practice to give Vitamin K to pregnant women to supplement the supply of this vitamin to the newborn baby. It is also customary for Vitamin K to be given to patients just before surgery to control bleeding as the result of the operation. It has been reported from recent studies that this vitamin may be used to prevent and treat cancer. It can aid in the preventing of heart failure and heart disease by preventing the arteries from hardening.
**Good sources**—Leafy green vegetables, alfalfa, egg yolks, yogurt, kelp, fish liver oils, safflower oil, soybean oil, oats, rye. And it is manufactured by certain bacteria in our own bodies in the intestines.
**Recommended daily intake**: RDA is 65—80 mcg. daily. Supplements are available in 100 mcg. doses.
**Toxicity**—500 mcg. is the recommended maximum.

**Vitamin P**—This vitamin, which is also known as bioflavonoid, is not always recognized as a vitamin. Vitamin P is needed for Vitamin C to be absorbed and function properly. It works with Vitamin C to keep connective tissues healthy. And it prevents the destruction of Vitamin C by oxidation. Vitamin P prevents bruises by strengthening the walls of capillaries. It fights inflammation and infections in the body.
**Good sources**—Paprika, blackberries, cherries, apricots, citrus fruit such as lemons, oranges and grapefruits.
**Recommended daily intake**: None is established. But nutritionists recommend 100 mg. for 500 mg. of Vitamin C taken.

**Toxicity**—No known toxic level

**Vitamin—Choline**: Choline is considered to be a part of the Vitamin B-complex group. This vitamin helps to prevent the build of bad cholesterol. It aids the memory by sending nerve impulses to the brain, fortifies the memory against loss in latter years and has proven to be helpful in the treatment of Alzheimer's disease. Choline aids the liver in eliminating drugs and poisons from the body.

**Good sources**—Eggs, leafy green vegetables, yeast, liver, whole grains, legumes.

**Recommended daily intake**: No RDA is established. Doses are usually 500—1,000 mg.

**Toxicity**—No known toxic level

**Vitamin—Folic Acid**: Folic acid is a part of the Vitamin B-complex group. This vitamin is essential in the production of DNA and RNA. It plays a vital role in the division and multiplication of cells. It is reported to aid in preventing birth defects and fight against intestinal parasites and food poisons. Folic acid is to prevent the growth of precancerous cells in the cervix, lung and colon. It is said to contribute to healthier looking skin. When taken with pantothenic acid and PABA, it may delay the graying of hair.

**Good sources**: Spinach, watercress, mustard greens, parsley, carrots, broccoli, mushrooms, soybeans, wheat germ, liver, milk, egg yolk, cantaloupe, apricots, avocados, pumpkins, sunflower seeds, beans and almost all green vegetable and herb leaves.

**Recommended daily intake:** The RDA is 180—200 mcg. daily. Supplements can be from 400 mcg. to 5 mg.

**Toxicity**: No known toxic level.

**Vitamin—Niacin**: Niacin is a part of the Vitamin B-complex group. Niacin plays a vital role in converting carbohydrates into energy for immediate use or storing it in an orderly fashion for future use. It supports a healthy digestive system and prevents gastrointestinal problems. This vitamin helps to raise the good cholesterol and lower the bad cholesterol. It improves circulation and aids in lowering high blood pressure. Niacin has been reported to help in cases of rheumatoid arthritis, osteoarthritis and joint pain. It is also good for the skin.

**Good sources**: Peanuts, wheat germ, whole barley, lean beef, lobster, haddock, stewed chicken, soybeans, whole bran, buttermilk, whole milk, collard greens, kale, turnip greens, potatoes, tomatoes, green peas, eggs, mushrooms, avocados, dates, figs, prunes.

**Recommended daily intake**: RDA is 13—19 mg. It can be found in doses from 50 to 1,000 mg.

**Toxicity**: Considered nontoxic, but can cause side effects with doses more than 100 mg.

**Vitamin—Pantothenic Acid**: This vitamin is considered to be a part of the Vitamin B-complex group and is also known as Vitamin B5. Pantothenic acid is vital to maintaining a healthy digestive system. It plays a vital role in supporting the adrenal glands to ensure proper secretion of adrenaline. This vitamin is essential for growth and aids in the conversion of carbohydrates and fats into energy. Pantothenic acid aids in detoxifying the body of herbicides, insecticides and drugs. It is said to help prevent wrinkles and the graying of the hair.

**Good sources**—Beef, pork, salt water fish, royal jelly honey, egg yolk, yeast, broccoli, molasses, peanuts, liver, corn, tomatoes, soy, whole grain, legumes.

**Recommended daily intake**: 10 mg. Supplements available in 10—300 mg.

**Toxicity**—No known toxic level

**Vitamin—Para-amino benzoic Acid (PABA)**: PABA is a part of the Vitamin B-complex group. This vitamin prevents the growth of many bacteria. PABA aids in the formation of red blood cells which are needed to carry oxygen throughout the body. It promotes smooth and healthy skin and prevents wrinkles. It can be used as an ointment to prevent sunburn and reduce sunburn pain and other pain from burns. PABA is said to maintain and restore the natural color of your hair.

**Good sources**: Liver, whole grains, rice, bran, wheat germ, molasses.

**Recommended daily intake**: None is established. Usually available in doses of 30-100 mg. to be taken three times a day.

**Toxicity**: No known toxic levels. However, it is not recommended to take high doses over an extended period of time.

# Other Essential Minerals

**Calcium**: Calcium is needed to develop and maintain strong bones and teeth. Calcium works with potassium and sodium to regulate the heartbeat. It plays a vital role in building muscles, including the heart muscle. Calcium aids in the impulse transmission of the nervous system and normalizes metabolism. It suggested that calcium helps to fight colon cancer.

**Good sources**: Cheese, milk, cream, cream, sea vegetation, nuts, collard greens, mustard greens, turnip greens, beet greens, kale, dried figs, celery, rutabagas, dates and raisins.

**Recommended intake**: RDA is 800—1,200 mg.

**Toxicity**: over 2,000 mg. daily

**Iron**: Iron is essential to the body for life and vitality. It produces red blood cells and certain enzymes. Iron promotes growth and prevents disease. Iron is needed to proper metabolize the B vitamins in the body.

**Good sources**: Liver, egg yolks, whole wheat, lean meat, oysters, dark chicken meat, spinach, nuts, sea vegetation, beans, dried apricots, dried peaches, prunes, raisins, parsnips, cauliflower, beets, blackberries, pineapple, sweet potatoes and iron-fortified cereal products.

**Recommended daily intake**: 3-10 mg. for children depending on age and size, 10-18 for adults and up to 30 mg. for pregnant women

**Toxicity**: Over 3 g. could be fatal for children. Precautionary measures should be taken to stay within recommended dosage to avoid iron overload which could lead to various health complications.

**Magnesium**: Magnesium is considered to be an anti-stress mineral. It contributes to a good night sleep and fights depression. Magnesium aids the cardiovascular system and decreases the risk of heart attacks. It helps to lower high blood pressure and helps in cases of angina. Magnesium is said to be helpful in cases of restless leg syndrome, migraine headaches, asthma, kidney stones, gallstones and calcium deposits.

**Good sources**: Figs, nuts, seeds, bananas, barley, corn, raisins, prunes, beef, fish, milk, oatmeal, raspberries, cherries, beets, dandelions, spinach, whole wheat, brown rice, cocoa, chocolate, dark green vegetables, beans, tofu, spinach, Swiss chard, halibut, mackerel, sunflower seeds and other seeds.

**Recommended daily intake**: 250—350 mg. for adults are recommended.

**Toxicity**: Up to 1,600 mg. can be taken along with a balance of 50% calcium intake at the same time.

**Manganese**: Manganese helps to activate the enzymes needed for the body to properly use biotin, B1 and Vitamin C. It is need for proper digestion, proper utilization of food and normal bone structure. Manganese aids in eliminating fatigue and improving memory.

**Good sources**: Whole grain cereals, herbs, nuts, beets, bananas, squash, celery, lettuce, kelp, asparagus, green leafy vegetables.

**Recommended daily intake:** The RDA is 2 mg. Supplements are usually 2—3 mg.

**Toxicity**: It is common for the vegetarian diet to exceed 20 mg. with no problem. Toxicity is more common from industrial sources.

**Phosphorus**: Phosphorus is very important for children because it plays a vital in the growth and repair of the body. It contributes to healthy bones, hair, teeth and gums. Phosphorus provides nourishment to the brain and helps to prevent mental fatigue.

**Good sources**: Fish, poultry, whole grains, nuts, egg yolk, pumpkin seeds, lean meat, oatmeal, corn meal, prunes, sea vegetation.

**Recommended daily intake**: RDA is 800—1200 mg.

**Toxicity**: No known toxic level.

**Potassium**: Potassium is essential for heart health. It works with sodium and as a diuretic to lower blood pressure, which will reduce your risk of heart attack and stroke. Potassium helps the body to dispose of its wastes. It aids in retaining elasticity of the tissues and helps to heal injured parts of the body.

**Good sources**: Citrus fruits, bananas, cantaloupe, tomatoes, watercress, all green leafy vegetables, mint leaves, sunflower seeds, potatoes, beans, asparagus, dates, raisins, cabbage, carrots, peaches, watermelon.

**Recommended daily intake**: The RDA is 3,500 mg. Inorganic potassium supplements are discouraged and can be fatal.

**Toxicity**: 18 grams

**Selenium**: Selenium works synergistically with Vitamin E as an anti-oxidant to slow the aging process and hardening of tissues. Studies have reported that it helps to fight prostate cancer, colon or rectal cancers and lung cancer. It is said to aid in cases of heart disease, angina, lupus and viral infections. Selenium relieves hot flashes and menopausal symptoms. It helps to keep the youthful elasticity of tissues.
**Good sources**: Tuna, lobster, clams, crab, cooked oysters, liver, wheat germ, bran, onions, tomatoes, broccoli, Brazil nuts.
**Recommended daily intake**: The RDA is 70 mcg. Supplements are available up to 200 mcg.
**Toxicity**: 5 mg.

**Sulfur**: Sulfur promotes healthy nails, skin and hair. It tones the skin and makes the hair strong and glossy. Sulfur helps the brain to function properly by maintaining the necessary oxygen level. It aids is fighting bacterial infections and helps the liver to secrete bile.
**Good sources**: Lean beef, fish, eggs, cauliflower, broccoli, cucumbers, corn, onion, turnips, sea vegetation, cabbage, beans.
**Recommended daily intake**: None is established.
**Toxicity**: No known toxic levels with organic sulfur, but is possible from the intake of large amounts of inorganic sulfur.

**Zinc**: Zinc directs and oversees the proper functioning of all enzymes and cells. It is vital for synthesizing protein and the formation of insulin. Zinc helps to support the proper acid-alkaline balance. It can help to correct taste and smell problems. It helps to heal internal and external wounds. Zinc has been reported to help in cases of prostate problems, lupus and rheumatoid arthritis.
**Good sources**: Red meat, liver, cooked oysters, clams, crab, fish, poultry, wheat germ, pumpkin seeds, eggs, yeast, ground mustard, beans.
**Recommended daily intake**: The RDA is 12—15 mg. for adults. Supplements are available in up to 60 mg.
**Toxicity**: 2 grams can have a toxic effect.

# Nutrition Glossary

This glossary gives you some of the nutritional value in the common fruits, vegetables, nuts and seeds that we eat. The information here only scrapes the surface of the live giving and healing qualities of these foods.

**Acai Berries**—Acai berries are high in antioxidants. They are a great source of potassium, calcium, fiber, Vitamin B1, Vitamin B2, Vitamin B3 and Vitamin C. They have anti-aging properties.

**Almonds**—Almonds are high in protein and a great source of magnesium, potassium and phosphorus.

**Apples**—Apples are good for your liver, kidneys, the intestines, skin, fights inflammation of the bladder. They can help with arthritis, lung asthma conditions.

**Artichoke**—Artichokes are high in potassium and reported to aid in anemia, excessive acidity, diarrhea, rheumatism, halitosis, obesity, neuritis and glandular disorders.

**Avocado**—Very high in Potassium. Avocados aid in the treatment of stomach ulcers, inflamed intestines and colon.

**Banana**—Bananas are always recommended for heart patients because of their potassium. But this tasty fruit can aid in the treatment of stomach ulcers, colitis, diarrhea, hemorrhoids, and good for general energy.

**Beets**—This blood builder is recommended for inflammation of the kidneys and bladder. It has also been reported to be valuable in cases of constipation, liver ailments, inflammation of the intestines, skin disorders, obesity and menstruation problems.

**Beet Greens**—High in calcium, potassium and Vitamin A. They are richer in iron than spinach. These greens have been reported to help in cases of constipation, dysentery, skin disorders, gout obesity and gonorrhea. Because of its high oxalic acid content, an excess should be avoided.

**Blackberry**—Blackberries are considered to be a general tonic and blood cleanser. They are high in antioxidants have been recommended for constipation, obesity, weak kidneys, arthritis and skin disorders.

**Blueberries**—High in antioxidants and also a blood cleanser. They are recommended for constipation, obesity, menstrual disorders and poor skin complexion.

**Broccoli**—Very high in Vitamin A, calcium and potassium. This cruciferous vegetable is excellent to aid in cases of obesity, constipation, high blood pressure and general digestion.

**Cabbage**—The cabbage is highly recommended as a blood cleanser and eye strengthener. They are also recommended for the teeth, gums, hair, nails, skin, obesity and kidney and bladder disorders. It is reported that fresh raw cabbage juice heals stomach ulcers.

**Cantaloupe**—High in Vitamin A and potassium. Cantaloupe has been reported to aid where there is a fever, high blood pressure, obesity, rheumatism, arthritis, kidney and bladder disorders and blood deficiencies.

**Carrots**—The carrot is one of the best miracle foods on earth! They are one of the highest sources of Vitamin A. Whether eaten whole or as a juice, they recommended in cases of obesity, toxemia, asthma, poor complexion, inflamed kidneys and bladder, high blood pressure, colitis, peptic ulcers and poor teeth. They help to improve the appearances of hair, nails and skin. It is recommended for nursing mothers to enhance the quality of their breast milk. They also help to prevent infections of the eyes, throat, tonsils, the sinus area and the lungs and lung passages.

**Cashew Nuts**—Great source of protein. Cashews are great body builders. They are recommended in cases of emaciation, problems with teeth and gums. The fat in the cashew is the same as in the heart and it is recommended to eat at least seven per day to help maintain a healthy heart.

**Cauliflower**—Blood purifier, high blood pressure, asthma, kidney and bladder disorders, obesity, gout, bad complexion, hair, bleeding gums.

**Celery**—Celery has been recommended for diseases of the kidney, arthritis, rheumatism, asthma, high blood pressure, pyorrhea, diabetes and dropsy.

**Chard**—High in Vitamin A and calcium. Chard has been recommended in cases of anemia, constipation, catarrh and obesity. Chard contains oxalic acid which is important in maintaining the eliminative organs. It is best to eat this vegetable raw because when cooked the oxalic acid is converted to an inorganic state that is destructive to the calcium in the body.

**Cherries**—Cherries are valuable in cases of anemia, poor complexion, bad blood, catarrh, constipation, cramps, obesity, worms, high blood pressure, rheumatism and asthma. They are effective cleansers of the liver and kidneys.

**Chickpeas**—Better known as garbanzo beans, these are an excellent source of protein and phosphorus.

**Coconut**—The coconut destroys tapeworms developed from eating meat. It helps to prevent thyroid problems and is recommended for constipation and gas build up in the stomach.

**Collards**—High alkaline content and in Vitamin A, Vitamin C and calcium. These greens are recommended in cases of anemia, liver trouble, acidosis, rheumatism, constipation, neuritis, arthritis, obesity, colon and aiding to eliminate drug poisoning from the body. They are said to cause colon cancer cells to commit suicide.

**Corn**—Corn is good for your pancreas and a good source of Phosphorus. Corn is recommended in treating anemia, constipation, emaciation and as a general body builder.

**Cranberry**—Cranberries can be beneficial in cases of skin disorders, high blood pressure, constipation, obesity, poor appetite and fevers. Cranberries or cranberry juice is recommended for kidney, liver or bladder disturbances.

**Cucumber**—The cucumber is a natural diuretic. It helps to digest proteins, helps to regulate blood pressure. The sulfur content helps to promote hair growth.

**Dandelion Greens**—Extremely high in Vitamin A and a great source of calcium. This vegetable has been recommended for cleansing of the liver, gallbladder and the spleen. They have also been recommended for anemia, low blood pressure, poor circulation, constipation and eczema.

**Dates**—Extremely high in potassium. Dates have been found to be beneficial in cases of anemia, low blood pressure, stomach ulcers, pyorrhea, tuberculosis and are recommended for nursing mothers.
**Eggplant**—Great source of potassium. Eggplant has been found to be valuable in cases of constipation, colitis, stomach ulcers and various nervous conditions.

**Fig**— Figs have been proven to be helpful in cases of constipation, low blood pressure, anemia, colitis, asthma, tuberculosis, pleurisy, catarrh, gout, rheumatism and skin diseases.

**Garlic**—Garlic is a miracle herb that can be eaten or taken in capsule form. It is a blood cleanser and is helpful with high blood pressure. It has been proven to be beneficial in cases of the common cold, asthma, chronic catarrh, bronchitis, fevers, gas, hardening of the arteries, thyroid hypo-function, sinusitis and promotes the expectoration of phlegm and mucus.

**Grape**—The grape is a great blood and body builder and is a source of quick and natural energy. It is reported to be helpful in cases of constipation, gout, the kidneys, rheumatism, skin and liver disorders.

**Guava**—High is Vitamin C. The guava is indicated in cases of diarrhea, prolonged menstruation, high blood pressure, poor circulation, acidosis, asthma, catarrh and obesity.

**Honeydew Melon**—This melon is a natural diuretic which makes them good for the kidneys. It is reported to be helpful in cases of obesity, rheumatism and poor complexion.

**Kale**—Very high in Vitamin A, calcium and Vitamin C. Kale is reported to be helpful in cases of constipation, obesity, acidosis, poor teeth, pyorrhea, arthritis, gout, rheumatism, skin diseases and bladder disorders.

**Kelp**—Another miracle food! Extremely high in Vitamin C. Either fresh or powdered, kelp is the richest source of organic iodine. It is reported to help correct mineral deficiencies and helps to offset deficiencies of an inferior diet. Kelp is valuable in overcoming poor digestion, preventing and overcoming goiter, and rebuilding and maintaining the proper function of all the glands.

**Kiwi**—It has been reported that the kiwi prevents asthma. It has been helpful in preventing wheezing and coughing. It is full of antioxidants and vitamins. It is also been report to help inhibit the development of colon cancer because the amount of fiber it contains.

**Kumquat**—The kumquat has been reported that this member of the orange family is helpful in cases of obesity, high blood pressure, catarrh, fevers and pneumonia.

**Leeks**—This valuable herb has some of the same medicinal properties of garlic. It is a general stimulant and reported to be helpful in cases of bronchitis, influenza, insomnia and low blood pressure.

**Lemon**—While the lemon is rich in nutrition, it is even richer in medicinal qualities. Lemon juice applied externally on cuts will destroy harmful bacteria. It can be applied directly to the skin to correct acne, eczema and erysipelas. Lemon juice has been recommended to improve wrinkles. Just apply lemon juice directly to the wrinkle, allow to dry and remove with coconut or olive oil. Use this same technique on blackheads, open sores and tan spots on the body. Apply directly to skin to relieve the itch of insect bites or irritation caused by poison oak or ivy. To relieve coughs, take a tablespoon of a lemon juice and honey half and half mixture every two hours. Gargle every hour with lemon juice and water half and half mixture to relieve a sore throat. To fight obesity drink one-half cup lemon juice and one half cup of water mixture before breakfast that will assist the body in the digestion of food and tend to prevent the accumulation of fatty deposits. When taken in large quantities, lemons have been reported to be helpful in cases of liver ailments, asthma, colds, fevers, headaches, pneumonia, rheumatism, arthritis and neuritis.

**Lentils**—Excellent source of protein and phosphorus. Lentils are recommended in cases of low blood pressure, anemia and emaciation.

**Lettuce**—Reported to be helpful in cases of anemia, constipation, insomnia, nervousness, catarrh tuberculosis, obesity, circulatory diseases, gout, poor appetite, urinary tract diseases, rheumatism, arthritis, hair.

**Lime**—The lime is valuable for cases of arthritis, scurvy and some liver ailments. It may be used as an antiseptic in the same manner at the lemon.

**Macadamia**—Has a significant supply of calcium, phosphorus and iron. It is excellent for body building and helpful in conditions of anemia and general energy.

**Mango**—Excellent source of Vitamin A. This fruit has proven to be helpful in cases of inflammation of the kidneys, other kidney ailments, acidity, poor digestion and clogged pores of the skin.

**Mushroom**—Should be cooked before consumed. There are many different mushrooms that have great health benefits that include preventing cancer and fighting heart disease.

**Mustard Greens**—Very high in Vitamin A, calcium and potassium. This powerful vegetable is an excellent tonic which is valuable for anemia, constipation, rheumatism, arthritis, acidity, kidney and bladder ailments and bronchitis.

**Nectarines**—This valuable fruit aids in digestion and relieves abdominal gas. It is recommended in cases of high blood pressure, asthma, rheumatism and bladder ailments.

**Noni**—We can enjoy the benefits of noni in the form of a juice. It is a good source of Vitamin C, Vitamin E, Vitamin B1, Vitamin B12, fiber and potassium. It is said to be beneficial in cases of arthritis pain, high cholesterol and digestion problems

**Okra**—Great source of potassium and calcium. This vegetable is recommended in cases of stomach ulcers, pleurisy, colitis, sore throat conditions and obesity.

**Olive**—It has been reported that olive oil stimulates contractions of the gall bladder, which makes it valuable for many kinds of gall bladder ailments. Olives have been found to help with liver disorders and helpful in cases of diabetes, abdominal gas and indigestion problems. The oil can be used externally on skin and hair.

**Orange**—Excellent source of Vitamin C, calcium and potassium. Oranges have been reported to be helpful in cases of asthma, bronchitis, tuberculosis, pneumonia, rheumatism, arthritis and high blood pressure. The consumption of orange juice has been found to help curb the desire of alcohol for those addicted. It also said to reduce hunger pangs and food cravings for suffering from obesity.

**Papaya**—Significant source of Vitamin A and potassium. This is an excellent fruit to fight obesity. The papaya contains the digestive enzyme papain which aids in digestion. It digests easily and cleanses the digestive tract. Papaya juice aids in relieving infections in the colon and has a tendency to break down pus and mucus reached by the juice.

**Parsley**—Very high in Vitamin A, Vitamin C and calcium. Parsley is not just for decoration. It is highly nutritious valuable in cases of anemia, inflammation of kidneys, tuberculosis, halitosis, menstruation disorders, fevers, dropsy, congested liver, congested gall bladder, diseases of the urinary tract, rheumatism, arthritis, acidosis, obesity, high blood pressure, catarrh, dyspepsia and treatment of venereal diseases.

**Peach**—High in Vitamin A and potassium. Peaches have proven valuable in cases of anemia, constipation, bronchitis, asthma, nephritis, high blood pressure, gastritis, acidosis and kidney and bladder stones. Helps to improve skin and add color to complexion.

**Peanuts**—High in protein, calcium and potassium. Great for energy and to treat low blood pressure.

**Pear**—Great source of potassium This fruit has been proven to help with poor digestion, constipation, high blood pressure, obesity, inflammation of the kidneys, nephrititis, acidosis, skin and conditions of the colon.

**Peas**—Great source of potassium. Peas are recommended to treat anemia, low blood pressure and to reduce cholesterol. They are excellent for nourishment and building and restoring strength.

**Pecans** Great source of protein, calcium, phosphorus and potassium. Pecans help with low blood pressure, boosts energy and great nourishment for teeth.

**Pepper, green**—High in Vitamin C and good source of potassium. The bell-shaped green peppers are valuable for liver disorders, obesity, constipation, high blood pressure and acidosis. The smaller red peppers have been found to helpful for colds, asthma, inflamed sinuses, malaria and for destroying intestinal worms.

**Persimmons**—Great source of Vitamin A and potassium. This fruit is excellent for energy and is valuable in cases of stomach and intestinal ulcers. It has been recommended in cases of pleurisy and sore throat conditions.

**Pine nuts**—Very high in phosphorus. This is an excellent food for body building, strength and energy.

**Pineapple**—This fruit is one of the best to eat for weight loss. It contains papain, which aids digestion and get rid of excess weight. Pineapples have been valuable in cases of goiter, dyspepsia, bronchitis, catarrh, high blood pressure and arthritis. Fresh pineapple juice expels intestinal worms.

**Pistachio**—Great source for protein. This nut is reported to be helpful in cases of low blood pressure, low vitality and can aid in the development of teeth, bones and general body building.

**Plum**—This fruit is recommended in cases of liver disorders, constipation, hemorrhoids, poor digestion, abdominal gas, obesity, bronchitis, tumors and skin eruptions.

**Pomegranate**—This is a powerful fruit has a cleansing and cooling effect on the system. The pomegranate is a good blood purifier and is reported to be helpful in relieving liver congestion, arthritis, obesity, high blood pressure and prostate cancer.

**Potato, sweet**—Very high in Vitamin A and potassium. This tasty vegetable is easily digestible, good for stomach ulcers and inflamed conditions of the colon. It is good for individuals engaged in heavy muscular work, persons suffering from low blood sugar and from poor blood circulation.

**Potato, white**—Great source of potassium. This versatile vegetable is good for body-building and is easily digested when baked.

**Prunes, dried**—Good source of Vitamin A and very high in Potassium. Prunes are recommended to increase vitality, improve the blood circulation, to treat hemorrhoids and constipation.

**Pumpkin**—High in Vitamin A and potassium. This fruit is valuable in cases of dropsy, inflamed intestines, stomach ulcers and hemorrhoids.

**Pumpkin seeds**—Very, very high in phosphorus and great source of protein. The high level of phosphorus in these seeds makes them helpful in nourishing the brain, good teeth and hair health.

**Radish**—This vegetable has been said to be helpful for the teeth, gums, nerves, hair and nails. They have been reported to relieve cases of constipation, catarrh, obesity and help to dissolve gallstones. Radishes have a mild diuretic effect that assist in regulating blood pressure.

**Raisins**—Great source of potassium, calcium and phosphorus. Raisins have been reported to be helpful in cases of tuberculosis, low blood pressure, anemia, emaciation and heart disease.

**Raspberries**—This fruit has been reported to be valuable for destroying body worms and removing excess fat. Raspberries are recommended for cases of constipation, high blood pressure and congested liver. Raspberries and raspberry tea have the effect of relieving menstrual cramps.

**Rice, Brown**—This grain is said to be beneficial to the hair, teeth, nails, muscles and bones. Brown rice is recommended for body building, stomach or intestinal ulcers and relief of diarrhea.

**Rutabagas**—The rutabagas recommended in cases of constipation, to remove gas from the stomach and the removal of intestinal worms.

**Sesame seeds**—Very high in calcium, potassium and phosphorus. This seed is helpful in cases of constipation, for ridding the body of pus formations, to cure liver ailments and the removal of worms from the intestinal tract. They are recommended to clear away the milk-like crust that forms on the face and head of infants.

**Soybeans**—Very high in protein, potassium and phosphorus. Soybeans are helpful for skin disorders, especially eczema. Soybeans are high in alkaline and are excellent for diabetics. The phytoestrogen content are helpful to combat some of the inconveniences of menopause.

**Spinach**—Very high in Vitamin A and potassium. Spinach is recommended in cases of anemia, constipation, neuritis, nerve exhaustion, tumors, insomnia, arthritis, obesity, high blood pressure, bronchitis and chronic indigestion. It is said to be helpful for ailments of the kidneys, bladder and liver. The nutrients in spinach make spinach helpful in preventing arteriosclerosis or hardening of the arteries.

**Squash, summer**—Great source of potassium. Summer squash is helpful in cases of high blood pressure, obesity, constipation and for bladder and kidney disorders.

**Squash, winter**—High in Vitamin A and potassium. The winter squash is helpful in cases of diarrhea, hemorrhoids, inflammation of the colon and ulcerations of the stomach and intestines. Because of the Vitamin A content, the winter squash should dissolve kidney, bladder and gallstones and prevent these stones from forming. This also makes them valuable for healthy skin, hair and improving the eyesight.

**Squash seeds**—These seeds are said to have the same nutritional value as pumpkin seeds.

**Strawberries**—Good source of calcium and postassium. This fruit is considered to be a skin cleanser and to rid the blood of harmful toxins. They are recommended for a sluggish liver, gout, rheumatism, constipation, high blood pressure catarrh and skin cancer.

**Sunflower seeds**—Very high in iron and protein. This nutty tasting seed nourishes the whole body because it supplies it with many vital elements needed for growth and repair. The sunflower seed recommended for weak eyes, poor fingernails, tooth decay, arthritis and dryness of skin. The oil from this seed is soothing to the skin and a good hair dressing.

**Tamarind**—This fruit is excellent when used as a laxative and as a diuretic remedy for bilious disorders, jaundice, and catarrh.

**Tangelo**—This fruit has most of the same health benefits as tangerines.

**Tangerines**—Good source of potassium and calcium. This tart fruit has been reported to be helpful in cases of obesity, bronchitis, pneumonia, rheumatism, arthritis, asthma, catarrh, diabetes, high blood pressure and various skin ailments. They have proven to be helpful for reducing fevers and for relieving conditions of congestion of the liver.

**Tapioca**—Tapioca are recommended for stomach and intestinal ulcers. It is beneficial for diarrhea and inflammation of the colon.

**Tomato**—Good source of Vitamin A and potassium. This fruit is recommended for cases of obesity, gout, rheumatism, tuberculosis, high blood pressure, and sinus trouble. They help reduce cholesterol in the blood, help to prevent hemorrhages and relieve gas in the stomach. They are said to improve the skin and purify the blood. The tomato is a natural antiseptic. They protect against infection and aid in dissolving gallstones.

**Turnip**—Great source of potassium. The root of turnips are recommended for constipation, tuberculosis, tuberculosis, insomnia and to relieve nervousness. When eaten raw they are reported to be good for the teeth and gums.

**Turnip greens**—Very high in Vitamin A and calcium. This vegetable that is rich in vitamins and minerals are good for persons suffering from anemia, poor appetite, tuberculosis, obesity, high blood pressure, bronchitis, asthma, liver ailments, gout and bladder disorders. They are also said to purify the blood, reduce acidity, destroy bacterial toxins in the bloodstream and improve the complexion.

**Walnuts**—High in phosphorus, potassium, calcium and protein. Walnuts help with constipation and liver ailments. They help to improve the body's metabolism and are excellent for muscle building. They are beneficial to the teeth and gums.

**Water Chestnuts**—Water chestnuts are recommended in cases of constipation, gas, worms and intestinal putrefaction.

**Watercress**—Very high in Vitamin A and calcium. Watercress is reported to be helpful in cases of eye disorders, obesity, bleeding gums, arthritis, rheumatism, hardening of the arteries and kidney and liver disorders.

**Watermelon**—Very high in potassium. Watermelon is highly recommended to help correct abnormal kidney conditions. The cucurbocitrin in the seeds can help to reduce high blood pressure.

**Wheat**—Wheat has been reported to be helpful in cases of arthritis, rheumatic fever, and perhaps some types of cancer.

# Herbs and Spices

The information on all of the herbs and spices below are inclusive of them as fresh, dried or ground herbs and spices.

**Allspice**—This herb has anti-inflammatory, antiseptic and anesthetic properties. It is said to aid in the digestive process and can help in cases of diarrhea. In sufficient qualities, it is a good source of potassium, manganese, iron and magnesium. This spicy herb should be avoided by individuals with stomach ulcers, ulcerative colitis or diverticulitis conditions.

**Basil**—Basil is very high in Vitamin K and is a good source of iron, calcium, manganese, magnesium, potassium, Vitamin A, Vitamin C and dietary fiber. It has been proven to have anti-inflammatory and anti-bacterial and aids in cardiovascular health.

**Bay leaves**—This aromatic herb has been known to help settle the stomach and treat digestive disorders. It is said to help breakdown and digest proteins. Bay leaves are reported to be an anti-inflammatory, anti-oxidant, anti-bacterial and anti-fungal. They have phytonutrients that aid in resistance against different types of cancers, in particular, cervical cancer. They are also known to provide protection against cardiovascular disease and help in cases of arthritis.

**Cayenne pepper**—The fiery cayenne pepper is very high in Vitamin A. It is a good source of manganese, dietary fiber and Vitamins C, B6 and K. It has a high concentration of a substance called capsaicin which has many healing qualities. Capsaicin has been shown to reduce blood cholesterol, lower blood pressure, reduce pain and clear congestion. A tea made with cayenne pepper is said to quickly stimulate the mucus membranes lining the nasal passages to drain, helping to relieve congestion and stuffiness. Cayenne pepper can prevent stomach ulcers by stimulating the cells lining the stomach to secrete protective buffering juices that prevent ulcer formation. Studies have shown this spicy herb to fight prostate, lung and pancreatic cancers.

**Cilantro**—This refreshing herb is packed with many life giving nutrients. Cilantro has anti-oxidant, anti-inflammatory, anti-fungal and anti-septic properties. It is an excellent source of Vitamins K and A. It is also a good source of potassium, iron and manganese. Cilantro is reported to increase HDL, the good cholesterol, and it decreases LDL, the bad cholesterol. It aids in digestion, helps to balance blood sugar level. Cilantro has shown to reduce menstrual cramps and detoxify the body.

**Cinnamon**—This delightful spice is very high in manganese and is a good source of dietary fiber, iron and calcium. Cinnamon has anti-oxidant, anti-inflammatory and anti-fungal properties. It controls the blood sugar levels when added to a dish that is high in carbohydrates. Research has shown that it boosts brain activity when consumed or smelled. Studies proved that the consumption of cinnamon reduced the proliferation of leukemia and lymphoma cancer cells. Cinnamon is said to support colon health. When combined with honey, cinnamon reduces cholesterol, settles an upset stomach and aids in relief from the common cold. Studies have shown that patients given one half teaspoon of cinnamon with honey experienced significant relief from arthritis pain after one week and were able to walk without pain within one month.

**Coriander**—This herb is a good source of dietary fiber, manganese, iron and magnesium. It is referred to as the "anti-diabetic plant. Studies have proven that coriander lowers blood sugar levels. The phytochemicals in this herb have shown to lower bad cholesterol and increase the good cholesterol. These phytochemicals also protect against urinary tract infections and cancer. Coriander has anti-inflammatory and anti-bacterial properties. Tests have shown that this herb fights Salmonella.

**Cumin**—Cumin is a very good source of iron. Research has shown that it may stimulate the secretion of pancreatic enzymes that are necessary for proper digestion and nutrient assimilation. Studies suggest that cumin has cancer fighting properties.

**Curry**—Curry powder is a combination of many different spices such as coriander, cumin, garlic, ginger, fenugreek, red pepper, black pepper and many other spices. The combinations vary according to that specific blend. With the very common ingredients that are listed, you may refer to that particular spice for their particular nutritional benefit.

**Garlic**—Because of how powerful garlic is in nutrition, it should be used as much as possible. It makes any bland dish tasty and healthy. It is an excellent source of Vitamin B6, Vitamin C and manganese. Garlic has anti-inflammatory, anti-bacterial, anti-oxidant, anti-oxidant and anti-viral properties. Routinely eating garlic has an effect on the lining of the blood vessel walls which causes them to relax; thus helping to reduce the risk of heart attack and stroke. Studies have shown that garlic does not lower bad cholesterol. But it does perform some of the same functions as the good cholesterol by preventing plaques caused by bad cholesterol. Garlic helps to lessen the amount of free radicals in the blood stream. Garlic has bee proven to fight cancer. And it is particularly even more powerful when combined with onion. Studies have shown that the garlic and onion combination fights such cancers as oral cavity, pharynx, esophageal, colorectal, laryngeal, breast, ovarian, prostate, renal and colon cancers. It has been report to reduce the cancer causing toxins created when grilling meats. So, use garlic liberally when grilling for great taste and great health.

**Ginger**—This tasty and versatile spice is a good source of potassium, manganese, magnesium and Vitamin B6. Studies have proven that ginger is beneficial in cases of digestive ailments, reducing gas, morning sickness and motion sickness. Tests have found it to be helpful in reducing inflammation associated with arthritis and aging knees. Extensive studies revealed cancer fighting qualities with colorectal and ovarian cancers. It is also an immune booster that can aid in fighting colds.

**Mint**—Mint is enriched with Vitamins A, C and B12. It also renders manganese, potassium, iron and selenium. Mint is a powerful anti-oxidant and has anti-bacterial properties. Research has proven it protects the body against the formation of cancerous cells. It is a blood cleanser. Mint eases and unblocks the breathing and respiratory passages. It can help to relieve symptoms of indigestion.

**Mustard**—The mustard spice, which is derived from mustard seeds, is a great source of selenium and magnesium. It contains phytonutrient compounds that are protective against gastrointestinal cancer and colorectal cancer. Studies have shown that mustard seeds inhibit the growth of existing cancer cells of protective against the formation of such cells.

**Nutmeg**—This herb has antibacterial and anti-inflammatory properties. It is used to improve memory and contains myristicin which inhibits an enzyme in the brains that contributes to Alzheimer's disease. Nutmeg oil can be used to treat toothaches. The seeds can be ground to make a paste to treat acne and eczema. Nutmeg should be used in moderation because of the possible damaging affects of toxic levels.

**Onion**—Onions are reported to be valuable for the hair, nails, eyes, asthma, bronchitis, pneumonia, influenza, colds, low blood pressure, insomnia, neuritis, vertigo, obesity. Heavy consumption can improve tuberculosis conditions.

**Oregano**—Oregano is an excellent source of Vitamin K. And it is a good source of iron, manganese, dietary fiber, omega 3 fatty acids, calcium and Vitamins A and C. It contains many phytonutrients that proven to also function as antioxidants that can help prevent oxygen-based damage to cell structures throughout the entire body. Oregano also has strong antibacterial properties.

**Parsley**—This very popular herb is very high in Vitamin A, Vitamin C and calcium. Parsley is not just for decoration. It can be very valuable in cases of anemia, inflammation of kidneys, tuberculosis, halitosis, menstruation disorders, fevers, dropsy, congested liver, congested gall bladder, diseases of the urinary tract, rheumatism, arthritis, acidosis, obesity, high blood pressure, catarrh, dyspepsia and treatment of venereal diseases.

**Pepper, Black**—Black pepper is a good source of manganese and Vitamin K. When black pepper hits your taste buds, it sends a message to your stomach to increase hydrochloric acid which helps to digest proteins and prevent the formation of intestinal gas. It has anti-oxidant and anti-bacterial properties. Black pepper stimulates the breakdown of fat cells and is a diuretic.

**Rosemary**—Rosemary is enriched with dietary fiber, iron and calcium. This herb contains phytochemicals that stimulate the immune system, increases circulation and improve digestion. It has unique anti-inflammatory properties that are reported to reduce the severity of asthma attacks. This herb increases blood flow to the head and brain that result in improving concentration. Rosemary is said to help increase the activity of detoxification enzymes. Studies proved that it inhibited the development of breast and skin cancer tumors in animals.

**Sage**—Research has confirmed that sage is an outstanding memory enhancer. Because it reduces inflammation, it is recommended in cases of arthritis, atherosclerosis and asthma. Sage also has anti-oxidant qualities.

**Salt**—Salt is a spice that we have to be very careful because of the sodium content. The recommended daily allowance of sodium is 2400 mg., which is equivalent to a teaspoon of salt. Too little sodium can also cause health issues. It is suggested that we aim for between 1500 and 2400 mg. for optimal health. When seasoning, I suggest adding salt last. It will enhance the blend of the flavors already in your dish and bring the flavors alive.

**Tarragon**—Tarragon is a good source of Vitamin A and potassium. This herb supports cardiovascular health. Studies have shown tarragon helps to inhibit blood platelet aggregation, adhesion and secretion. It has hyperglycemic properties that help to control blood sugar. It is a natural anesthetic and diuretic. Tarragon contains the cancer fighting agent, caffeic acid, which has the ability to cleanse the body of free radicals and kill viruses.

**Thyme**—Thyme is an excellent choice as a source of Vitamin K. It is also a good source of manganese, iron, calcium and dietary fiber. It has anti-oxidant and anti-bacterial properties. Research has proven that it also has cancer preventive properties. It has proven to be helpful in cases of chest and respiratory problems including coughs, bronchitis and chest congestion.

**Turmeric**—This subtle and powerful herb is a good source of manganese, iron, Vitamin B6, dietary fiber and potassium. It has anti-inflammatory and antioxidant properties. Many studies have been conducted with turmeric with amazing results. It has shown to be effective in treating rheumatoid arthritis and cystic fibrosis. Research has revealed that this herb has promising results in preventing numerous cancers and inhibiting the growth and spread of numerous cancers. When turmeric is prepared with onions, it is effective against colon cancer. And when it is combined with cruciferous vegetables, such as cauliflower, broccoli or kale, turmeric rendered compelling results in the fight against prostate cancer. Curcumin which is a powerful phytonutrient found in turmeric that lowers the bad cholesterol and increases the good. This powerful substance also inhibits the development of Alzheimer's disease.

# Oils

When cooking with oils, it is very important to check on what the smoke point is for that oil. It is usually marked on the label. When you heat oil past its smoke point, it is then broken down into a substance that can be very unhealthy and possibly cause cancer. Oils with a low smoke point are good for salads or baking at the limited temperature. Refined oils usually have a higher smoke point, but have been stripped of some of the nutritional value. Beware of refined, hydrogenated and enriched oil which means they have been processed to insure a long shelf life. And that could mean that it is not good for you. I have listed the unrefined smoke points according to my references. But rely on what is on the label of the oil that you purchase.

**Almond oil**—Almond oil is high in potassium and protein. It has laxative properties.
**Smoke Point:** 420° F.

**Avocado oil**—This mild and buttery tasting oil is a good source of potassium. Cold pressed avocado oil renders Vitamins B, C and E. Studies show that it helps to lower bad cholesterol.
**Smoke Point:** 520° F.

**Canola oil**—This oil is a source of omega 3-fatty acids and Vitamin E.
**Smoke Point:** 225° F.

**Coconut oil**—Coconut oil is good for heart and liver health. It increases the metabolism to assist with energy and weight loss. It fights bacteria, fungus and viruses in the body.
**Smoke Point:** 350° F.

**Corn oil**—Corn oil is a source of omega 6 fatty acids.
**Smoke Point:** 320° F.

**Flaxseed oil**—This oil has a low smoking point. Flaxseed oil is a great source of omega-3 fatty acids, protein and fiber. It is a natural laxative

and has anti-viral, anti-bacterial, anti-fungal and anti-cancer properties. Studies have shown that it is helpful in cases of arthritis and lupus.
**Smoke Point:** 225° F.

**Extra Virgin Olive oil**—It is always best to buy the 'virgin" or "extra virgin" olive oil. Olive oil has been reported to be helpful in cases of ulcers, gastritis, heart disease and high cholesterol. It has a quality in it that releases the healing phytochemicals in plant food into the body.
**Smoke Point:** 320° F.

**Grape seed oil**—Grape seed oil is high in Vitamin E and is considered to be very heart healthy.
**Smoke Point:** 420° F.

**Hazelnut oil**—Hazelnut oil is very heart healthy. Recent studies showed that it reduced the risk of heart attacks by 50%. It is a good source of Vitamin E and Vitamins B1, B2 and B6.
**Smoke Point:** 420° F.

**Peanut oil**—Peanut oil is a favorite oil for high temperature cooking. It contains Vitamin E. But after a recent study, it come into question regarding this oil contributing to heart disease.
**Smoke Point:** 440° F.

**Safflower oil**—Safflower oil is rich in omega 6 fatty acids. It is a source of Vitamin E.
**Smoke Point:** 510° F.

**Sesame oil**—Sesame oil has anti-bacterial properties. It is rich in nutrients such as Vitamin E, calcium, magnesium and iron. Sesame oil is said to lower cholesterol and reduce the risk of heart disease.
**Smoke Point:** 410° F.

**Soybean oil**—Soybean oil is rich in both omega 3 and omega 6 fatty acids.
**Smoke Point:** 495° F.

**Sunflower oil**—Sunflower oil is rich in omega 6 fatty acids. It is a source of Vitamin E.
**Smoke Point:** 440° F.

**Walnut oil**—Walnut oil is an antioxidant and has anti-cancer properties. It is a good source of manganese, melatonin and omega-3 fatty acids. Walnut oil is very heart healthy because it can help to prevent plaque build up in the arteries.
**Smoke Point:** 320° F.

# Eating for Healing

The foods listed with each of these conditions can be eaten for prevention and to enhance your healing with the treatment that you receive from your physician.

**Anemia**—Apples, apricots, artichokes, barley, beets, black walnuts, blackberries, blueberries, brazil nuts, broccoli, Brussels sprouts, cabbage, cauliflower, chard, cherries, collard greens, corn, dandelion greens, dates, endives, figs, grapefruit, guava, horseradish, kale, kelp, lemons, lettuce, macadamia nuts, mustard greens, oranges, parsley, peaches, peanuts, pecans, pepper, prunes, raisins, spinach, soybeans, tomatoes, turnip greens, watercress.

**Arthritis**—Asparagus, beans, beets, blackberries, cantaloupe, carrots, cherries, collard greens, cucumbers dandelion greens, endives, grapefruit, kale, mustard greens, okra, oranges, parsley, pineapple, pomegranate, pumpkins, spinach, strawberries, sunflower seeds, tangerines, turnips, wheat.

**Asthma**—Apples, apricots, barley, cabbage, carrots, cauliflower, celery, cherries, elderberries, endives, figs, garlic, guava, horseradish, lemons, nectarines, onions, oranges, peaches, peppers, raisins, tangerines, turnips, turnip greens.

**Bladder ailments**—Apples, beets, cabbage, cantaloupe, cauliflower, cranberries, horseradish, kale, mustard greens, nectarines, spinach, summer squash, turnip greens and all leafy green vegetables.

**Blood pressure, high**—Barley, broccoli, cantaloupe, carrots, cauliflower, celery, cranberries, cucumbers, garlic, guava, kumquats, nectarines, oranges, parsley, peaches, pears, peppers, pineapple, raspberries, spinach, summer squash, strawberries, tangerines, tomatoes, turnip greens, mustard greens.

**Blood pressure, low**—Barley, black walnuts, brazil nuts, cucumbers, dandelion greens, dates, figs, hickory nuts, leeks, onions, peanuts, peas, pecans, pistachio nuts, sweet potatoes, pumpkin, raisins, soybeans.

**Blood purifiers**—Blackberries, blueberries, cabbage, garlic, mint, pomegranate juice, raspberries, strawberries.

**Bone weakness**—Grapefruit, guava, horseradish, kale, lemons, oranges, parsley, peppers, pistachios, rice, spinach, tomatoes, turnip greens, watercress, wheat.

**Bronchitis**—Apricots, asparagus, beans, beet greens, broccoli, cabbage, cantaloupe, carrots, corn, dandelion greens, dates, elderberries, endives, garlic, kale, leeks, lettuce, mustard greens, onion, orange, papaya, parsley, pecans, peaches, peas, pineapple, plum, sweet potatoes, prunes, spinach, tangerines, turnip greens, watercress.

**Cartilages, weak**—Broccoli, Brussels sprouts, cauliflower, collard greens, grapefruit, guava, horseradish, kale, lemons, oranges, parsley, peppers, spinach, tomatoes, turnip greens, watercress.

**Cataracts**—Apples, beets, blueberries, broccoli, cabbage, carrots, coconuts, collard greens, dandelion greens, grapefruit, lemons, lettuce, peanuts, prunes, turnips watercress.

**Colds**—Apples, carrots, broccoli, Brussels sprouts, cauliflower, collard greens, dandelion greens, elderberries, garlic, grapefruit, guava, horseradish, kale, lemons, onions, oranges, parsley, peppers, spinach, tomatoes, turnip greens, watercress.

**Conjunctivitis**—Apples, apricots, asparagus, beans, beet greens, blueberries, broccoli, cabbage, cantaloupe, carrots, coconuts, collard greens, corn, dandelion greens, endives, grapefruit, kale, lemons, lettuce, mustard greens, orange, papaya, parsley, peaches, peanuts, peas, pecans, sweet potatoes, prunes, spinach, turnip greens, watercress.

**Constipation**—Apples, apricots, avocado, barley, beans, beets, blackberries, blueberries, broccoli, Brussels sprouts, cabbage, cantaloupe, carrots, cauliflower, celery, chard, cherries, collard greens, dandelion greens, dates, eggplant, elderberries, endives, figs, grapes, kale, lettuce, mustard greens, oats, onions, peaches, peanuts, pears, peas, pecans, peppers, persimmons, pineapple, plum, prunes, pumpkin seeds, raisins, raspberries, rutabagas, sesame seeds, soybeans, spinach, summer squash, strawberries tomatoes, turnips, walnuts, water chestnuts.

**Dandruff**—Apples, beets, blueberries, broccoli, cabbage, carrots, coconuts, collard greens, dandelion greens, grapefruit, lemons, lettuce, peanuts, prunes, turnips, watercress.

**Diarrhea**—Artichoke, bananas, barley, blackberries, blueberries, collard greens, corn, guava, kale, mushrooms, oranges, parsnips, peanuts, peas, potatoes, sweet potatoes, raspberries, rice, soybeans, winter squash, tapioca, tomatoes, turnip greens.

**Diabetes**—Cabbage, celery, cilantro, cinnamon, coriander, dandelion greens, endive, olives, parsley, soybeans, strawberries, tangerines, tarragon.

**Digestion aid**—Apples, black pepper, cayenne pepper, cherries, garlic, grapefruit, horseradish, kelp, lemons, papayas, peaches, pears, pineapple, plums.

**Ear infections**—Cantaloupe, carrots, corn, dandelion greens, endives, kale, lettuce, mustard greens, papayas, parsley, peaches, peas, pecans, prunes, spinach, sweet potatoes, turnip greens, watercress.

**Eczema**—Cabbage, corn, dandelion greens, eggs, lemons, soybeans.

**Emotional upsets**—Apples, ginger.

**Energy loss**—Apricots, asparagus, barley, beans, beet greens, black walnuts, broccoli, Brussels sprouts, cabbage, cantaloupe, carrots, cauliflower, collard greens, corn, dandelion greens, endives, grapefruit, guava, horseradish, kale, lemons, lettuce, mustard greens, oranges, papayas, parsley, peaches, peanuts, peas, pecans, peppers, prunes, soybeans, spinach, sweet potatoes, tomatoes, turnip greens, watercress.

**Eyesight, improvement of**—Apples, beets, blueberries, broccoli, cabbage, carrots, coconuts, collard greens, dandelion greens, grapefruit, lemons, lettuce, onions, peanuts, prunes, turnips watercress.

**Fatigue**—Barley, beans, cabbage, corn, oats, peas, rice, rye, wheat.

**Gallstones**—Apples, apricots, celery, dandelion greens, grapefruit, olives, parsley, radishes, tomatoes, winter squash.

**Gout**—Beet greens, blackberries, cabbage, cauliflower, cherries, figs, grapes, kale, lettuce, strawberries, tomatoes.

**Gum problems**—Broccoli, Brussels sprouts, cauliflower, collard greens, grapefruit, guava, horseradish, kale, lemon, orange, parsley, pepper, spinach, tomatoes, turnip greens, watercress.

**Hair**—Apples, apricots, asparagus, beets, blueberries, broccoli, cabbage, carrots, coconuts, collard greens, dandelion greens, dandelion greens, grapefruit, lemons, lettuce, oats, onions, peanuts, prunes, radishes, rice, winter squash, watercress.

**Joint pain**—Broccoli, Brussels sprouts, cauliflower, cauliflower, collard greens, grapefruit, guava, horseradish, kale, lemons, noni juice, oranges, parsley, peppers, spinach, tomatoes, turnip greens, watercress.

**Kidneys, help for**—Asparagus, avocado, beets, cabbage, cantaloupe, celery, cranberries, dandelion greens, grapes, mangos, olives, parsnips, peanuts, radishes, spinach, summer squash, strawberries, watercress, watermelon.

**Liver, help for**—Asparagus, beans, beets, broccoli, cabbage, carrots, cauliflower, corn, cucumbers, dates, lemons, lettuce, limes, olives, onions, parsley, peaches, pomegranates, potatoes, raisins, raspberries, sesame seeds, spinach, strawberries, tangerines, tomatoes, turnip greens, walnuts, watercress.

**Menstruation, irregular**—Barley, beans, beets, blackberries, blueberries, corn, lettuce, parsley, peas, raspberries, rice, soybeans.

**Menopausal distress**—Flaxseed, flaxseed oil, soy, sweet potatoes, yams, foods with Zinc.

**Muscles, weakness of**—Apricots, asparagus, barley, beans, beet greens, black walnuts, brazil nuts, broccoli, cabbage, cantaloupe, carrots, corn, dandelion greens, lettuce, mustard greens, oranges, papayas, parsley, peaches, peanuts, peas, pecans, sweet potatoes, prunes, soybeans, spinach, turnip greens, watercress.

**Muscle pain**—Barley, black walnuts, brazil nuts, peanuts, peas, pecans, soybeans.

**Finger nails and toe nails**—Apples, beets, blueberries, broccoli, cabbage, coconuts, carrots, collard greens, cucumbers, dandelion greens, grapefruit, lemons, lettuce, oats, onions, parsnips, peanuts, prunes, radishes, rice, sunflower seeds.

**Nervousness**—Almonds, avocado, barley, beets, cabbage, collard greens, corn oil, dates, eggplant, kale, lettuce, mushrooms, peanuts, peas, potatoes, rice, soybeans, tomatoes, turnip greens.

**Obesity**—Apples, artichokes, beets, blackberries, blueberries, broccoli, Brussels sprouts, cabbage, cantaloupe, carrots, cauliflower, celery, chard, cherries, collard greens, grapefruit, guava, honeydew melon, kale, kumquat, lemons, lettuce, mustard greens, nectarines, okra, onions, oranges, parsley, pears, peppers, pineapple, plums, pomegranate, radishes, raspberries, spinach, strawberries, summer squash, tangerines, tomatoes, turnip greens, watercress.

**Osteoporosis**—Celery, dates, figs, kale, mustard greens, raisins, rutabagas, sesame seeds, turnip greens.

**Pancreas**—Cumin, cabbage, corn.

**Pneumonia**—Prunes, spinach, sweet potatoes.

**Pyorrhea**—Apples, celery, chestnuts, cucumbers, dates, kale, lemons.

**Rheumatism**—Artichokes, asparagus, blackberries, cantaloupe, celery, cherries, collard greens, cucumbers, dandelion greens, figs, grapes, honeydew melon, kale, kelp, lettuce, mustard greens, nectarines, oranges, parsley, strawberries, tangerines, tomatoes, watercress.

**Scalp**—Apricots, asparagus, beans, beet greens, broccoli, cabbage, cantaloupe, carrots, corn, dandelion greens, endives, kale, lettuce.

**Scurvy**—Broccoli, Brussels sprouts, cauliflower, collard greens, grapefruit, guava, horseradish, kale, lemons, limes, oranges, parsley, peppers, spinach, tomatoes, turnip greens, watercress.

**Skin**—Acorns, apples, beet greens, blackberries, blueberries, broccoli, cabbage, cantaloupe, carrots, cauliflower, cherries, coconuts, collard greens, cranberries, dandelion greens, figs, grapefruit, grapes, kale, lemons, lettuce, peaches, peanuts, pears, prunes, tangerines, turnip greens, watercress.

**Stones, bladder**—Lemon juice, olive oil, peaches, radishes, winter squash.

**Stones, kidney**—Apple cider, apples, parsley, peaches, winter squash.

**Teeth enamel**—Apricots, asparagus, beans, beet greens, broccoli, cabbage, cantaloupe, carrots, corn, dandelion greens, endives, kale, lettuce, mustard greens, oranges, papaya, parsley, peaches, peas, pecans, prunes, spinach, sweet potatoes, turnip greens, watercress.

**Voice hoarseness**—Apricots, asparagus, barley, beans, beets greens, black walnuts, brazil nuts, broccoli, cabbage, cantaloupe, carrots, corn, dandelion greens, endives, kale, lettuce, mustard greens, oranges, papaya, parsley, peaches, peanuts, peas, pecans, prunes, soybeans, spinach, sweet potatoes, turnip greens.

**Vomiting, prevention**—Barley, cabbage, collard greens, corn, kale, mushrooms, peanuts, peas, potatoes, rice, soybeans, tomatoes, turnip greens, wheat germ.

**Worms, removal**—Apples, cherries, onions, peaches, peppers, pineapple, pomegranate, pumpkin seeds, raspberries, rutabagas, sesame seeds, water chestnuts.

## *Cancer fighting foods*

**Bladder cancer**: Blueberries, broccoli, Brussels sprouts, cabbage, carrots, cauliflower, cranberry juice, cumin, strawberries, water.
**Possible causes**: Caffeine, carbonated drinks, coffee, tobacco.

**Bone marrow cancer**: Apples, asparagus, beans, beef (lean), beef liver, beets, blackberries, blueberries, broccoli, cauliflower, coconut water, collards, dates, grapefruit, guava, high-folate foods, lentils, mustard greens, oranges, oysters, parsley, raisins, romaine lettuce, spinach, turnip greens.

**Possible causes**: I could not find a possible cause from any credible sources. However, to avoid it, I suggest maintaining a balanced diet with plenty of dark leafy green vegetables along with enough iron.

**Breast cancer**: Beans, blueberries, brown rice, carrots, chili peppers, cod, collard, dried prunes, flaxseed oil, foods with Vitamin D, garlic, ginger, grapefruit, grapes, herring, kale, lentils, mustard greens, nuts, olive oil, peas, rainbow trout, rosemary, salmon, sardines, seaweed and other sea vegetation, seeds (especially flaxseed), spinach, strawberries, tomatoes, turmeric, tuna, turnip greens, whole grains, raw fruit and vegetables.
**Possible causes**: Coffee, sodas, fat intake over 40% of calories, processed oils, refined oils, saturated fat.

**Colon or rectal cancers:** Apples, barley, beans, blackberries, broccoli, collard greens, cruciferous vegetables, flaxseed, garlic, ginger, grapes (black), green tea, kale, leeks, oatmeal, onion, oranges, pears, peas, raspberries, tomatoes (cherry), turmeric, wheat-bran cereals, whole grains, a high fiber diet fruits and vegetables, especially the red, purple and blue ones.
**Possible causes**: Fat intake over 40% of calories.

**Liver cancer**: Avocados, beans, broccoli, cruciferous vegetables, fish, grapes, green tea, milk, milk thistle, oatmeal, olive oil, pomegranate juice, squash, sweet potatoes, white meat, yams, yogurt.
**Possible causes**: Alcohol, animal fats, high fat meats, tobacco.

**Lung cancer**: Blueberries, carrots, cod, flaxseed, green tea, foods with Folic Acid, foods with Vitamin D, garlic, kale, leafy green vegetables, milk, peanuts, tomatoes, salmon, spinach.
**Possible causes**: Tobacco.

**Mouth cancer**: Carrots, collard greens, kale, mustard greens, tomatoes, turnip greens,
**Possible causes**: Alcohol, tobacco.

**Ovarian cancer**: Broccoli, cantaloupe, carrots (raw), collard green, corn, foods high in flavonoids, ginger, kale, oranges, spinach, tea, tomato sauce, yams.
**Possible causes**: High fat diet, smoking.

**Pancreatic cancer**: Broccoli, Brussels sprouts, cabbage, chili peppers, collard greens, corn, cruciferous vegetables, green tea, jalapenos, kale, tomatoes, tomato paste.
**Possible causes**: Coffee, high sugar diet, tobacco.

**Prostate cancer**: Brazil nuts, broccoli, Brussels sprouts, cabbage, carrots, cauliflower, cruciferous vegetables, garlic, ginger, green tea, kale, pomegranates, pomegranate juice, scallions, turmeric.
**Possible causes**: Infection or inflammation of the prostate, excessive amounts of red meat, excessive amounts of high fat dairy products, obesity, fat intake over 40% of calories, genetics, age, race.

**Skin cancer**: Blueberries, chili peppers, collard greens, dark chocolate, fatty fish, flaxseed, jalapenos, kale, mustard greens, rosemary, salmon, strawberries, tomatoes (cooked), turnip greens, dark colored fruits and vegetables.
**Possible causes**: Enriched white flour, foods with high sugar levels, genetics, ultraviolet radiation from the sun, white rice.

**Stomach cancer**: Beans, carrots, chili peppers, chives, garlic, grapes, green tea, jalapenos, leeks, onion, turmeric, green and yellow leafy green vegetables.
**Possible causes**: Smoked, salted and pickled foods.

**Throat cancer**: Beans, carrots, collards, folic acid foods, kale, mustard greens, peas, spinach, spinach, turnip greens.
**Possible causes**: Alcohol, smoking, oral sex.

**Overall cancer fighters**: Blackberries, carrots, cruciferous vegetables, cumin, foods rich in Vitamin B-complex group, garlic, ginger, oregano, rosemary, sweet potatoes, tapioca, tomatoes, turmeric.
**Possible causes**: Processed foods, smoked meats, processed meats, caffeine, food additives such as, BHA, BHT, red food dyes.

## *Foods for Heart Health*

**Lower bad cholesterol:** Apples, artichokes, avocados, blackberries, broccoli, Brussels sprouts, cauliflower, cayenne pepper, cilantro, cinnamon, citrus fruits, currant, garlic, grapes, green peppers, flaxseed, kale, lean meats, leeks, olives, onion, peas, psyllium, raspberries, salmon, sesame oil, spinach, tarragon, tomatoes, walnuts, walnut oil, watercress.

**Reduce high blood pressure:** allspice, almond, asparagus, avocado, beets, broccoli, cabbage, cantaloupe, carrots, cauliflower, celery, cayenne pepper, cherries, cinnamon, cucumber, curry, eggplant, flaxseed, garlic, guava, kumquat, mint, mustard greens, nectarines, okra, oranges, parsley, pears, persimmons, pecans, pineapple, pomegranate, prunes, pumpkin, radishes, raspberries, spinach, strawberries, tamarind, tangerines, tomatoes, turnip greens, watermelon, white potatoes.

**Improve Circulation:** Blackberries, blueberries, cayenne pepper, ginger, oranges, pomegranates, pomegranate juice, pumpkin seeds, strawberries, watermelon.

**Heart cells:** CoQ10

**Heart fat:** Pistachios (7 per day)

# Eating Plans

There are so many great diet plans out there that really work. I have catered my way of eating to giving my body nourishment needed to combat diseases. I do have fun and eat whatever I want from time to time. But I keep in mind what is going on in my body and make the changes that I need to stay healthy.

If we eat more raw vegetables, fruits, nuts, herbs and seeds, we fight all kinds of diseases from taking over our bodies. If you already have a health problem, you can develop an eating plan that will focus on giving your body what it needs to help it to heal itself. Be sure to discuss your plans with your physician.

*Each plan has a special purpose:*

**Eating Plan Number 1—Body Cleanse Diet—**Cleanses the colon, kidneys, gall bladder and liver.

**Eating Plan Number 2—Eliminating Diet—**Eliminates toxins and mucous from the body. This plan can be beneficial to individuals overcoming addictions.

**Eating Plan Number 3—Low Carb Diet—**This plan is designed to develop better eating habits. The carbohydrates are low enough to loose weight with exercise and give you enough energy to do what you need to do.

# Eating Plan Number 1

## *Body Cleanse Diet*

This eating plan is designed to cleanse your colon, liver, kidneys and gall bladder. The complete cleanse is for seven days. If you have any medical conditions or any concerns, please consult your physician before implementing this plan. This plan has been recommended by a medical doctor.

For the first three days you are to eat only raw fruits and vegetables to cleanse the colon. The menus below give you some ideas of how to plan your meals. You may prepare a couple of large salads to last all three days or different smaller salads daily. Eat raw fruits and vegetables liberally. On the first day you may take a natural laxative. Drink lots of water every day.

At the end of the third day do a coffee enema. If you have never done an enema before, check your local drug store for the supplies needed. Make a pot of caffeinated coffee, organic is recommended. Then follow the instructions from the kit that you purchase. Remember, this is your body! And you are to care of every part of it in order to keep your body healthy. If you take care of every part that has its purpose, it will take care of you.

The next two days are to cleanse the kidneys and gall bladder. And the last two days are to cleanse the liver.

**Day 1**
Colon

**Breakfast**
Drink ½ cup lemon juice and ½ cup warm water 30 minutes before breakfast.
1 bowl Oatmeal with Honey and Cinnamon

**Morning Snack**
Orange

**Lunch**
2 cups Pomegranate Salad

**Afternoon Snack**
1 Grapefruit

**Dinner**
2 cups Collard Green Salad

**Evening snack**
1 cup Strawberries and Raspberries

**Day 2**

**Breakfast**
Drink ½ cup lemon juice and ½ cup warm water 30 minutes before breakfast.
1 bowl Oatmeal with Honey and Cinnamon

**Morning Snack**
Grapefruit

**Lunch**
2 cups Strawberry Salad

**Afternoon Snack**
Peach

**Dinner**
2 cups Olive Salad

**Evening snack**
1 cup Blackberries and Blueberries

## Day 3

### Breakfast
Drink ½ cup lemon juice and ½ cup warm water 30 minutes before breakfast.

1 bowl Oatmeal with Honey and Cinnamon

### Morning Snack
Banana

### Lunch
2 cups Blueberry Salad

### Afternoon Snack
Pear

### Dinner
2 cups Sweet Potato Salad

### Evening snack
1 cup Pineapple

### Days 4 and 5
Kidney and Gall Bladder Cleanse

Kidney
1 Gallon of Organic Apple Cider each day
Drink one 8 oz. glass of apple cider every two hours until it is all gone. Be sure to drink a glass of water 30 minutes after drinking the apple cider. This is to cut the citric acid.

Gall Bladder Cleanse
½ cup of lemon juice and ½ cup olive oil each day
Shake well and drink just before going to bed. Sleep on your right side. The olive oil will make your bladder contract and remove any stones that could be forming.

**Days 6 and 7**
Liver

Drink 4 ounces of distilled water every hour.
Eat only vegetable soup all day that is prepared in a health way.

**After the Cleanse**
Drink fresh squeezed juices and lots of water for the next week after the cleanse.

# Eating Plan 2

## *Eliminating Diet*

This eating plan is designed to eliminate excess acids and mucus from the body. The five main organs for elimination are the skin, lungs, bowels, kidneys and liver.

To eliminate properly, it is suggested to eat three lemons, two grapefruits and six oranges daily. You should eat one large salad for lunch and one meal of properly cooked vegetables for dinner daily. You should drink plenty of water. You may drink plenty of grape juice, pomegranate juice, orange juice, grapefruit juice and organic unfiltered apple juice. Make sure all juices are 100% juice with no high fructose corn syrup.

Other suggested fruits are pineapple, peaches, cherries, plums, pears, apples, strawberries, raspberries, blueberries, blackberries and papaya. All fruits should be fresh and not canned or frozen. If possible, make sure that all fruits were ripe before being picked.

The best vegetables to eat are spinach, celery, carrots, parsley, tomatoes, asparagus, green onions, red cabbage, green cabbage, lettuce, cucumbers, radishes, okra, eggplant, kale and all dark leafy green vegetables.

Your bowels should completely evacuate at least two or three times daily. If that does not happen, you are experiencing constipation. In that case, you should cleanse your bowels once or twice a week with an herbal enema.

Only eat fruits and vegetables. You make snack on any of the fruits and vegetables liberally throughout each day. Do not eat starchy foods, white sugars, proteins, potatoes, cakes, dairy products and eggs.

Get plenty of oxygen by breathing deeply and exercising in the open air. Take baths daily while eliminating. Every other day take a bath using three pounds of Epsom salts in a tub full of water. While taking the bath, drink lots of water and massage the body. To increase circulation and activity of the skin, thoroughly massage the entire body with one half common salt and one half Epsom salt.

Eliminating for seven days is suggested. However, it can be more or less. The information that I am sharing here has been primarily gleaned from the book "Back to Eden" by Jethro Kloss. You may refer to this book for more helpful information.

Before starting any drastic change in your diet, be sure to check with your physician. You may want to start things slowly to see how your body responds. If you are on medication, you will need to have bread, oatmeal or something to offset the citric acid in the orange and grapefruit when taking your medicine.

## Day 1

**Breakfast**
Drink ½ cup lemon juice and ½ cup warm water 30 minutes before eating.
Three lemons juice should render ½ cup lemon juice.

2 oranges
1 grapefruit

**Lunch**

Olive Garlic Salad
1 orange

**Mid-day snack**
1 Orange

**Dinner**
2 cups Green cabbage and Tomatoes, cooked
1 Orange
1 Grapefruit

**Evening Snack**
1 Orange

**Day 2**

**Breakfast**
Drink ½ cup lemon juice and ½ cup warm water 30 minutes before eating.

2 Oranges
1 Grapefruit

**Lunch**
Pomegranate Salad
1 Orange

**Mid-day snack**
1 Orange

**Dinner**
2 cups Red cabbage and Tomatoes, cooked
1 Orange
1 Grapefruit

**Evening Snack**
1 Orange

## Day 3

### Breakfast
Drink ½ cup lemon juice and ½ cup warm water 30 minutes before eating.

2 Oranges
1 Grapefruit

### Lunch
Blueberry Salad
1 Orange

### Mid-day snack
1 Orange

### Dinner
2 cups Eggplant, baked
1 Orange
1 Grapefruit

### Evening Snack
1 Orange

## Day 4

### Breakfast
Drink ½ cup lemon juice and ½ cup warm water 30 minutes before eating.

2 Oranges
1 Grapefruit

### Lunch
Collard Green Salad
1 Orange

### Mid-day snack

1 Orange

**Dinner**
2 cups Okra and Tomatoes, cooked
1 Orange
1 Grapefruit

**Evening Snack**
1 Orange

## Day 5

**Breakfast**
Drink ½ cup lemon juice and ½ cup warm water 30 minutes before eating.
Three lemons juice should render ½ cup lemon juice.

2 Oranges
1 Grapefruit

**Lunch**
Strawberry Salad
1 Orange

**Mid-day snack**
1 Orange

**Dinner**
2 cups Cauliflower, cooked
1 Orange
1 Grapefruit

**Evening Snack**
1 Orange

## Day 6

**Breakfast**

Drink ½ cup lemon juice and ½ cup warm water 30 minutes before eating.

2 Oranges
1 Grapefruit

**Lunch**
Mustard and Spinach Salad
1 Orange

**Mid-day snack**
1 Orange

**Dinner**
2 cups Broccoli
1 Orange
1 grapefruit

**Evening Snack**
1 Orange

**Day 7**

**Breakfast**
Drink ½ cup lemon juice and ½ cup warm water 30 minutes before eating.

2 Oranges
1 Grapefruit

**Lunch**
Pineapple Spinach Salad
1 Orange

**Mid-day snack**
1 Orange

**Dinner**

2 cups Asparagus, cooked
1 Orange
1 Grapefruit

**Evening Snack**
1 Orange

# Eating Plan 3

## *Low Carb Diet*

The low carb diet is one of the easiest diets to follow and continue as a way of life. This plan is designed to give you the six to nine servings of fruits and vegetables that you need daily along with lots of protein while keeping the carbs low. This is just a suggested format for you to follow. I personally prefer to prepare a large quantity of my main entrees, vegetables and salads at the beginning of the week to last me several days. If you prefer to do the same, you may use one day's menu for one week and try them all in that manner. After you have tried them all, customize your own low carb menu and make this a way of life.

**Day 1**

**Breakfast**
Shrimp and Artichoke Scramble

**Mid-Morning Snack**
½ cup Strawberries

**Lunch**
Chicken Breast
Avocado and Walnut Salad

**Mid-Day Snack**
1 String Cheese

5 Almonds

**Dinner**
Baked Tilapia
Broccoli cooked with onion and garlic

**Evening Snack**
Tangerine

**Day 2**

**Breakfast**
Breakfast Kale Wrap

**Morning snack**
½ Grapefruit

**Lunch**
Pan Fried Salmon
Mustard Greens and Pear Salad

**Afternoon snack**
Celery and Cream Cheese

**Dinner**
Spicy Roasted Chicken
Kale

**Evening Snack**
1 cup Strawberries

**Day 3**

**Breakfast**
1 Slice Whole Wheat Toast
1 teaspoon Peanut Butter
½ Grapefruit

**Morning Snack**
½ cup Cucumber slices
1 slice Swiss Cheese

**Lunch**
Grilled Halibut
Pineapple Spinach Salad

**Afternoon Snack**
½ Apple

**Dinner**
Boneless Skinless Chicken Thighs
Collard Greens

**Evening Snack**
½ Apple

**Day 4**

**Breakfast**
Southwest Scramble
2 slices of Tomato

**Morning Snack**
Tangerine

**Lunch**
Tuna Salad (whichever version you prefer)

**Afternoon Snack**
½ cup Pomegranate Seeds and Pecans

**Dinner**
Steak with Onions and Mushrooms
Steamed Broccoli

**Evening snack**

½ cup Sugar Free Yogurt

## Day 5

### Breakfast
Kale and Sun-dried Tomato Scramble

### Morning Snack
½ cup Blueberries

### Lunch
Grilled Halibut
Cabbage

### Afternoon Snack
1 Turkey slice with Cream Cheese

### Dinner
Pork Loin (roasted with garlic and black pepper)
Kale

### Evening Snack
1 cup Blackberries

## Day 6

### Breakfast
1 slice of Whole Wheat toast
Spinach and Artichoke Scramble

### Morning Snack
Peach

### Lunch
Turkey Breast
2 cups Mustard Greens and Pear Salad

### Afternoon Snack

10 Almonds

**Dinner**
Zesty Okra with Chicken

**Evening Snack**
1 cup Raspberries

**Day 7**

**Breakfast**
1 Slice Whole Wheat Toast
Cucumber and Tomato Scramble

**Morning Snack**
1 boiled Egg
1 slice Low Fat Cheddar Cheese

**Lunch**
Shrimp (sautéed in olive oil and garlic)
2 cups Olive Salad

**Afternoon Snack**
½ Apple

**Dinner**
Lemon Chicken
Mustard Greens

**Evening Snack**
½ Grapefruit

# Customizing Your Personal Eating Plan

When customizing your personal eating plan, be sure to keep in mind what your personal health needs and goals are. I have put together an Eating Plan Worksheet to make it easier for you to reach your goals. You may copy this to use as much as you like.

| Meal Plan Worksheet | | | | | | | |
|---|---|---|---|---|---|---|---|
| **Date:** | | | | | | | |
| **Meal** | **Fruit** | **Veggies** | **Fiber** | **Protein** | **Iron** | **Carbs** | **Fat** |
| **Breakfast** | | | | | | | |
| Snack | | | | | | | |
| **Lunch** | | | | | | | |
| Snack | | | | | | | |
| **Dinner** | | | | | | | |
| Snack | | | | | | | |
| **Totals** | | | | | | | |
| **Weight Goal:** | | | | | | | |
| **Weight Today:** | | | | | | | |
| **Total Lost:** | | | | | | | |
| **Balance Remaining:** | | | | | | | |

It is recommended that we eat from 6 to 9 servings of fruits and vegetables per day. For the average person, we should have 25 grams of fiber and at least 50 grams of protein per day. The need for more protein increases with your size.

To lose weight, it is recommended that we bring our fat intake down to around 30 grams. The suggested carbohydrate allowance is 300 grams. However, to lose weight, the low 100's would be the goal to shoot for.

## *Super Foods*

**This is a list of super foods that we should include in our diets on a regular basis, getting them in our systems every week.**

| | |
|---|---|
| Apples | Broccoli |
| Beans | Carrots |
| Blackberries | Cauliflower |
| Blueberries | Cilantro |
| Cinnamon | Parsley |
| Collard Greens | Pomegranates |
| Curry Powder | Pumpkin seeds |
| Eggs | Salmon |
| Flaxseed oil | Spinach |
| Flaxseeds | Sunflower seeds |
| Garlic | Sweet Potatoes |
| Ginger | Tomatoes |
| Kale | Turmeric |
| Lemons | Turnip Greens |
| Olive oil | Walnuts |
| Lean beef | |

# Notes

# Notes

_____
_____
_____
_____
_____
_____
_____
_____
_____
_____
_____
_____
_____
_____
_____
_____
_____
_____
_____
_____
_____
_____
_____
_____
_____
_____
_____
_____
_____
_____

# Notes

# Notes

# References

Encyclopedia of Fruits, Vegetables, Nuts and Seeds for Healthful Living by Joseph M. Kadahs, Ph. D.

Back to Eden by Jethro Kloss

Earl Mindell's Vitamin Bible by Early Mindell

Healing Without Medication by Robert S. Rister

Cooksmart by Lucy Doncaster


http://www.whfoods.com/genpage.php?tname=foodspice&dbid

http://www.indepthinfo.com/ginger/health-benefits.shtml

http://completewellbeing.com/article/a-nutty-affair/

http://health.learninginfo.org/oregano.htm

http://www.nutrition-and-you.com/allspice.html

http://www.helpwithcooking.com/herb-guide/bay-leaves.html

http://lifestyle.iloveindia.com/lounge/benefits-of-bay-leaf-7544.html

http://www.cayennepepper.info/health-benefits-of-cayenne-pepper.html

http://ezinearticles.com/?Four-Clinical-Studies-Prove-Cayenne-Pepper-Kills-Cancer-Cells&id=815652

http://healthmad.com/alternative/10-miraculous-health-benefits-of-honey-and-cinnamon-combo/

http://www.vegetarian-nutrition.info/herbs/coriander.php

http://www.cancure.org/cancer_fighting_foods.htm

http://www.nutricaplabs.com/tarragon-health-benefits.aspx

http://food-facts.suite101.com/article.cfm/mint_a_powerful_antioxidant

http://www.vegetarian-nutrition.info/herbs/thyme.php

http://www.nutrition-and-you.com/cilantro.html

http://www.elook.org/nutrition/herbs/1277.html

http://www.mayoclinic.com/health/vitamin-d/ns_patient-vitamind

http://health.learninginfo.org/benefits-of-vitamin-k.htm

http://www.ehow.com/about_5371670_food-sources-vitamin-p.html

http://www.nutritional-supplements-health-guide.com/what-is-pantothenic-acid.html

http://www.anyvitamins.com/vitamin-b5-pantothenic-info.htm

http://www.springboard4health.com/notebook/min_magnesium.html#Toxicity

http://www.vitaminstuff.com/paba.html

http://www.cancure.org/cancer_fighting_foods.htm

http://www.foxnews.com/story/0,2933,193441,00.html

http://findarticles.com/p/articles/mi_m1189/is_6_280/ai_n30985740/

http://findarticles.com/p/articles/mi_m1077/is_12_55/ai_65572101/

http://www.time.com/time/magazine/article/0,9171,990837,00.html

http://nutrition.suite101.com/article.cfm/foods_that_fight_cancer

http://www.telegraph.co.uk/news/uknews/1560769/Dark-fruit-and-veg-may-fight-colon-c ancercells.html

http://www.ehow.com/about_5059439_foods-nonsmall-cell-lung-cancer.html

http://www.life123.com/health/nutrition/cancer-prevention/liver-cancer-treatment.shtml

http://www.lifescript.com/Health/Conditions/Cancer/10_Foods_That_Help_Fight_Cancer.aspx

http://www.webmd.com/cancer/news/20060405/tea-may-fight-ovarian-breast-cancers

http://women.webmd.com/ovarian-cysts

http://www.wrongdiagnosis.com/p/pancreatic_cancer/causes.htm

http://www.diseaseproof.com/archives/cancer-green-veggies-fight-pancreatic-cancer.html

http://www.healthdiaries.com/eatthis/10-foods-that-fight-prostate-cancer.html

http://www.cancer.org/docroot/CRI/content/CRI_2_2_2X_What_causes_prostate_cancer_36.asp

http://www.ehealthmd.com/library/skincancer/SC_causes.html

http://ezinearticles.com/?Eat-Foods-That-Fight-Skin-Cancer&id=2844229

http://www.nutraingredients.com/Research/Leeks-and-chives-fight-stomach-cancer

http://www.mayoclinic.com/health/stomach-cancer/ds00301/dsection=causes

http://www.newscientist.com/article/dn11819

http://www.whfoods.com/genpage.php?tname=nutrient&dbid=63

http://www.cookingforengineers.com/article/50/Smoke-Points-of-Various-Fats

http://avocadopoint.com/avocados/Avocado+Oil/

http://www.buzzle.com/articles/almond-oil.html

http://www.recipetips.com/glossary-term/t—36190/almond-oil.asp

http://www.whfoods.com/genpage.php?tname=foodspice&dbid=81

http://www.bodybuildingforyou.com/health-supplements/flax-seed-oil.htm

http://www.alive.com/6854a17a2.php?current_topic=35

http://www.brighthub.com/health/diet-nutrition/articles/36952.aspx

http://www.home-remedies-for-you.com/articles/282/nutrition/health-benefits-of-hazelnut.html

http://www.askdrsears.com/html/4/t043800.asp

http://www.buzzle.com/articles/sesame-oil-nutrition-facts.html

http://www.highbloodpressureinfo.org/food-for-high-blood-pressure.html

http://www.lifescript.com/Body/Food/Good-foods/3_Terrific_Uses_For_Coconut_Milk

http://www.whfoods.com/genpage.php?tname=foodspice&dbid=55

http://www.fabulousfoods.com/index.php?option=com_resource&controller=article&category_id=224&article=19943

http://www.nutrition-and-you.com/cilantro.html

http://nutrition.about.com/od/fruitsandvegetables/p/blackeyedpeas.htm

http://www.livestrong.com/thedailyplate/nutrition-calories/food/generic/red-bell-pepper-raw/

http://www.nutrition-and-you.com/oregano.html

http://www.healthcentral.com/peoplespharmacy/408/61202.html

http://mushroominfo.com/benefits/

http://lifestyle.iloveindia.com/lounge/benefits-of-onion-1565.html

http://nutrition.about.com/od/fruitsandvegetables/p/cilantro.htm

http://www.nutrition-and-you.com/basil-herb.html

http://www.buzzle.com/articles/balsamic-vinegar-health-benefits.html

http://www.pyroenergen.com/articles09/green-onions-scallion.htm

http://www.homeremediesweb.com/apple_cider_vinegar_health_
benefits.php

http://www.livestrong.com/article/85032-nutrition-spaghetti-squash/

http://www.ehow.com/how_2383476_benefit-from-bay-leaf.html

http://www.ilovepecans.org/nutrition.html

http://www.organicfacts.net/health-benefits/vegetable/health-benefits-
of-broccoli.html

http://lifestyle.iloveindia.com/lounge/benefits-of-pomegranate-1841.
html

http://www.organicfacts.net/nutrition-facts/animal-products/
nutritional-value-of-beef-and-pork.html

http://www.healthdiaries.com/eatthis/10-health-benefits-of-avocados.
html

http://www.prohealth.com/library/showarticle.cfm?libid=8326

http://nutritiondata.self.com/facts/fruits-and-fruit-juices/1825/2

http://www.netrition.com/rdi_page.html

http://www.nutrientfacts.com/AlmanacPages/Potassium_
Recommended_Daily_Allowance_RDA.htm

http://www.homeremediesweb.com/turmeric-health-benefits.php

http://www.ehow.com/facts_5626583_acai-berry-supplement.html

# Other Nutritional Resources

Medline.com
Center for Disease Control
National Institute of Health
Nutrient Recommendation: Dietary Reference Intake (DRI)
American Dietetic Association
American Diabetic Association
American Cancer Society
American Heart Association
Journal of Clinical Nutrition